To:
Kirsty

IT'S ALL ABOUT
DINNER

Nicky Corbishley
Kyle Books

An Hachette UK Company
www.hachette.co.uk

First published in Great Britain
in 2022 by Kyle Books,
an imprint of Kyle Cathie Ltd
Carmelite House
50 Victoria Embankment
London EC4Y 0DZ
www.kylebooks.co.uk

ISBN: 9781914239397

Distributed in the US by
Hachette Book Group,
1290 Avenue of the Americas,
4th and 5th Floors,
New York, NY 10104

Distributed in Canada by
Canadian Manda Group,
664 Annette St., Toronto,
Ontario, Canada M6S 2C8

Publishing Director: Judith Hannam
Publisher: Joanna Copestick
Project Editor: Samhita Foria
Design: Helen Bratby
Production: Emily Noto

A Cataloguing in Publication record for this
title is available from the British Library

Printed and bound in Italy

10 9 8 7 6 5 4 3 2

Dedication

For Chris, who has been my number one supporter and business partner since we started this amazing food journey. From filming and editing our recipe videos, managing the company finances, implementing tech solutions, managing objective setting meetings, to taste testing mushroom-laden recipes (when he hates mushrooms), he's the best husband a girl could wish for. Also, for Gracey (main washer-upper) and Lewis (dish-washer emptier), thank you for being the best (and most brutally honest) taste testers.

Notes:

* All oven temperatures are for fan oven.
* Unless otherwise stated, salt is always regular table salt.
* Unless otherwise stated, pepper is always freshly ground black pepper.
* If soy sauce isn't listed as 'light' or 'dark' soy sauce, it means 'standard' soy sauce. You can use light soy sauce as a replacement if you don't have standard soy sauce.
* I use stock in a lot of my recipes. If you make homemade stock, that's great, but water + stock cubes will work just fine for any of the recipes.
* I use full-fat (whole) dairy (milk, cream, butter, yogurt, cheese) and full-fat coconut milk and coconut cream in my recipes. I find they taste better, and full-fat versions are a lot less likely to split when heating.

saturday

wednesday

tuesday

monday

thursday

friday

sunday

contents

Introduction

Some people say that breakfast is the most important meal of the day, but I wholeheartedly disagree. Dinner is the meal I think about the most, look forward to all day, and plan for, usually days in advance. If we're lucky, work and school are done for the day and it's the time to sit down with the family, relax and have a good catch-up. If we can sit at the table, then so much the better, but sometimes, dinner on a tray on our knees, in front of a good film, is perfect too.

I love the way dinner can take so many different forms.

* **Sunday dinner – a big family affair, with all the trimmings and a proper pudding that leaves you full to bursting.**
* **Super-fast weeknight dinners, when you've got to fit it in between work and after-school clubs.**
* **Friday night fake-away with a spicy curry or a delicious stir-fry.**
* **Date night, where you pull out all the stops to recreate some restaurant-style food, without having to worry about taxis or babysitters!**
* **Or something cooked long and slow – put in the slow cooker in the morning, so it's tender, tasty and filling the house with the most glorious aromas come dinner time.**

However you do dinner, I hope you'll find lots of recipes here that'll become family favourites, and your go-to, whatever the occasion.

Why should this book be on your recipe book shelf? *My Kitchen Sanctuary* website is my online cookery book, which I constantly add to. I've been testing, photographing and sharing recipes since 2014, and we've now got hundreds and hundreds of recipes on there!

I wrote this book to share the best of the best – the recipes that our readers constantly come back to. With a book, you can also flick through lovely photos and recipes for dinner inspiration, without any adverts or other distractions that can get in the way when you're looking at things online. Of course, I didn't want to only bring you existing recipes. So I've included a selection of brand-new recipes too. Recipes that I hope you'll love as much as I do.

My dream is for this book to be that well-thumbed, dog-eared, ingredient-spattered book that you always come back to when you're planning and making dinner.

Check out the videos!

Not only does each recipe in this book have a photo, but there is also a recipe video. I've included a QR code for every single recipe, which will take you through to a video, so you can see how the recipe is made, every step of the way.

About Nicky & *Kitchen Sanctuary*

Nicky grew up in Southport, before moving to Staffordshire, where she got her degree in Computing Science. After university, she spent 14 years in corporate IT, where she met husband Chris. They have two children, Gracey and Lewis. Food and cooking have been a passion for Nicky since age 11, when she first started cooking for her family.

She started *Kitchen Sanctuary* in 2014, initially to diarize her recipes, and as a way to relax after a long day at the office. The recipes proved popular with readers, and the site started to grow, eventually allowing Nicky to work on it full-time.

In 2017, Chris quit his corporate job to join Nicky to work on *Kitchen Sanctuary*, and that's when they started making recipe videos for their YouTube channel.

Kitchen Sanctuary is now one of the most popular recipe websites in the UK, with the readership in the millions every month. The *Kitchen Sanctuary* YouTube channel is also growing rapidly, with recipe videos being added every week.

Quick & easy.

As much as I love spending time cooking in the kitchen, having some quick dinners in my repertoire is an absolute necessity for those busy weekdays. However, I still want fresh, tasty meals that result in clean plates and smiling faces all round, even when I am short on time. My **Spicy sea bass** is ready in just 12 minutes, and the **Quick & easy chicken ramen** is on the table in just 20 minutes! Even if you're not a lover of blue cheese (like me!), try my **Gorgonzola pasta**. I first tried this recipe as a bit of an experiment, and now I'm a total convert. It really is comfort food in a bowl. The kids love the **Hunter's chicken** – which couldn't be simpler, with only 5 ingredients.

Gorgonzola pasta

A really simple yet decadent pasta dish made with an easy gorgonzola cream sauce and all topped off with fresh flat-leaf parsley and crunchy toasted walnuts. This really is rich, comforting bowl food, and it's ready in 20 minutes!

400g (14oz) penne pasta (or your favourite pasta shape)

2 tablespoons unsalted butter

1 banana shallot, peeled and finely chopped (or use ½ onion)

2 garlic cloves, peeled and minced

150ml (⅔ cup) double (heavy) cream

125g (4½oz) Gorgonzola cheese, crumbled or roughly chopped

2 tablespoons finely grated Parmesan

3 tablespoons chopped flat-leaf parsley

⅛ teaspoon salt

¼ teaspoon ground black pepper

to serve

1 tablespoon finely grated Parmesan

a pinch of ground black pepper

1 tablespoon chopped flat-leaf parsley

2 tablespoons chopped toasted walnuts (dry-fry them in a frying pan [skillet] for 1-2 minutes until lightly browned)

1. Cook the pasta in boiling water as per the cooking instructions, until al dente.

2. Melt the butter in a large frying pan (skillet) over a medium heat. Add the shallot and fry for 3-4 minutes, until softened.

3. Add the garlic and cook for a further minute.

4. Add the cream, Gorgonzola cheese, Parmesan, parsley, salt and pepper and stir until the Gorgonzola melts.

5. By this time, the pasta should be ready. Drain the pasta in a colander over the sink, reserving ½ cup of the cooking water.

6. Add the pasta to the pan with the cream sauce and toss together, using a set of tongs. Add in a splash of the pasta cooking water (or more) if you want to loosen up the sauce at all.

7. Divide the pasta among the plates. Top with Parmesan, black pepper, fresh parsley and toasted walnuts, then serve.

TIP Gorgonzola Dolce is best for this recipe – it provides that lovely creaminess. However, you can use Piccante if you like a slightly more pungent taste.

Quick & easy

8

Salmon en papillotte

Cooking salmon in little paper parcels with lots of fragrant ingredients is a great way to make a quick dinner that's a little bit different. The sauce in the parcels tastes amazing drizzled over rice.

2 teaspoons sunflower oil

1 teaspoon sesame oil

1 garlic clove, peeled and minced

1½ tablespoons light soy sauce

1½ tablespoons honey

2 skin-on salmon fillets

½ red (bell) pepper, deseeded and sliced

100g (3½oz) fresh baby corn

1 carrot, peeled and sliced into matchsticks

1 red chilli, sliced (deseed it if you don't want it too hot)

6 spring onions (scallions), sliced into thin strips

1 teaspoon mixed black and white sesame seeds

lime wedges, to serve

cooked rice, to serve

1. Preheat the oven to 200°C/400°F/gas mark 7.

2. In a small bowl, mix together the sunflower oil, sesame oil, garlic, soy sauce, and honey.

3. Take two large pieces of baking parchment, fold each one in half, and cut into a semi-circle. Unfold and place on a baking tray (sheet).

4. Place a salmon fillet , skin-side-down, inside each of the parchment circles, sitting them on the fold line.

5. Arrange the red pepper, baby corn and carrot around the salmon fillets.

6. Scrunch up the edges of the parchment circles a little (so the sauce doesn't run out) and spoon the soy mixture over the salmon fillets, then arrange the sliced chilli on top.

7. Bring the four corners of the parchment paper together and fold them over several times, then twist so the paper is completely sealed. Make sure there are no gaps for the sauce to escape from.

8. Place the baking tray (sheet) in the oven and cook for 18 minutes, until the salmon is tender.

9. Open up the parcels carefully (steam will escape) and sprinkle over the sliced spring onion and sesame seeds and nestle in a couple of lime wedges.

10. I like to serve the salmon, still in the paper, with rice. There will be some lovely flavourful liquid in the parcels, which tastes delicious, poured straight over the rice.

TIP Swap the salmon for your favourite chunky fish. Cod and lemon sole both work great.

Quick & easy

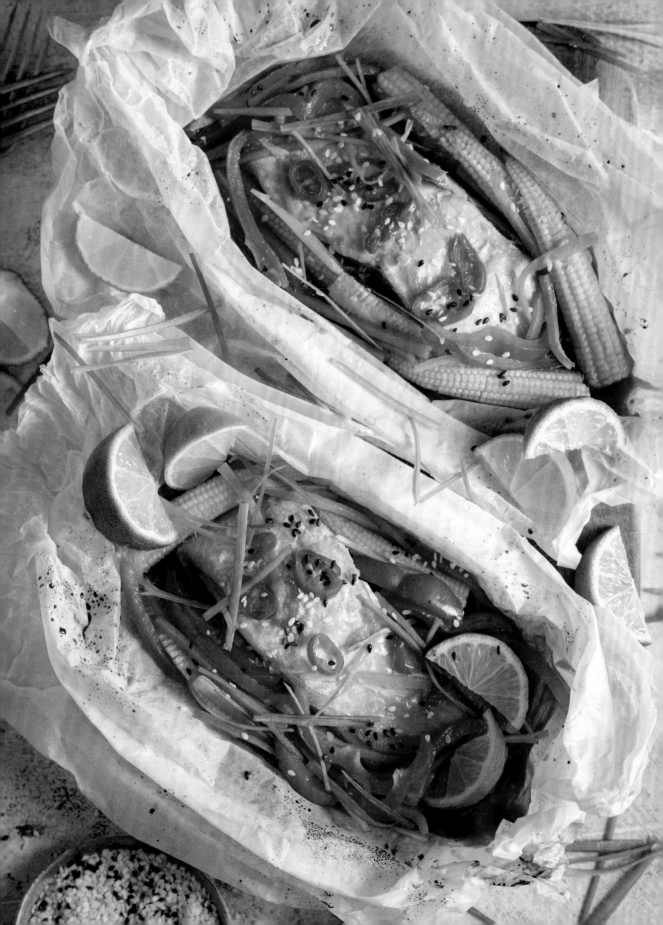

Honey-garlic-butter baked salmon

This is the easiest and best baked salmon recipe in the world! Stir a few simple ingredients together, pour over salmon fillets and bung it in the oven for 12-15 minutes. Done.

4 skin-on salmon fillets

2 tablespoons unsalted butter, melted

2 garlic cloves, peeled and minced

2 tablespoons honey

½ teaspoon dried parsley (or 2 teaspoons finely chopped fresh flat-leaf parsley)

¼ teaspoon salt

¼ teaspoon ground black pepper

a pinch of paprika

1 lemon, sliced into half-moons

1. Preheat the oven to 200°C/400°F/gas mark 7. Line a baking tray (sheet) with foil or a silicon mat.

2. Place the salmon fillets, skin-side-down, on the baking tray (sheet).

3. In a small bowl, mix together the melted butter, garlic, honey, parsley, salt, pepper and paprika.

4. Pour the mixture over the salmon fillets (don't worry about the sauce pooling on the tray).

5. Arrange the lemon slices on and around the salmon.

6. Place in the oven and bake for 8 minutes.

7. Open the oven and baste the salmon with any of the sauce that has pooled on the tray. Bake for a further 4–7 minutes, until the salmon is tender and cooked through.

8. Serve with your favourite vegetables.

TIP The leftover salmon tastes great, served cold, as part of a salad or in a wrap. Simply cool, cover and refrigerate the salmon, then flake it up before serving.

Quick & easy

12-minute spicy sea bass

Soft, flaky sea bass, drizzled in a sweet, spicy sauce and baked in the oven.
Super- quick and easy – ready in 12 minutes!

2 tablespoons sesame oil
1 red chilli, finely chopped
4 tablespoons honey
2 tablespoons dark soy sauce
½ teaspoon ground ginger
2 garlic cloves, peeled and minced
1 tablespoon lime juice
   (juice from ½ small lime)
4 skin-on sea bass fillets
½ teaspoon cornflour
   (cornstarch)
2 tablespoons light brown sugar

to serve
a handful of fresh coriander
   (cilantro), torn
a bunch of spring onions
   (scallions), sliced into thin strips
1 red chilli, thinly sliced
slices of lime

1. Preheat the oven to
200°C/400°F/gas mark 7.
2. In a small bowl, mix the oil, chilli,
honey, soy sauce, ginger, garlic and
lime juice.
3. Place the sea bass fillets,
skin-side down, on a baking
tray (sheet). Sprinkle over the
cornflour and gently rub it into
the fish.
4. Spoon over the honey-soy
sauce mix (it will pour off a little,
but that's fine).
5. Sprinkle over the sugar, then
place in the oven and cook for
8 minutes. Half-way through
cooking, open the oven and baste
the fish with the sauce in the tray
(it will be stickier now it's been in
the oven).
6. Once the fish is cooked, take
out of the oven and baste again
with the sauce, then sprinkle over
the coriander, spring onion and
slices of chilli.
7. Serve with lime slices.

TIP Go for skin-on fillets. The
skin will help the flesh hold
together and ensure the fish is
more tender.

Quick & easy

Cajun cod with smoky potato wedges

We're letting the oven do most of the work with this simple, slightly spicy fish dinner. No searing or par-boiling required, the potato wedges and the cod are simply coated in spices and oil, then baked until tender.

smoky potato wedges

500g (1lb 2oz) floury white potatoes, sliced into wedges (no need to peel)

½ teaspoon salt

½ teaspoon ground black pepper

½ teaspoon smoked paprika

¼ teaspoon garlic powder

¼ teaspoon chilli (red pepper) flakes

2 tablespoons olive oil

cajun cod

4 cod fillets

2 tablespoons Cajun spice mix

¼ teaspoon salt

¼ teaspoon ground black pepper

2 tablespoons olive oil

to serve

a simple green salad

1. Preheat the oven to 200°C/400°F/gas mark 7.

2. Arrange the potato wedges on a large baking tray (sheet).

3. Sprinkle over the salt, pepper, smoked paprika, garlic powder and chilli flakes and toss together to coat the potatoes.

4. Drizzle the potatoes with the olive oil, toss again to coat evenly, then place in the oven for 20 minutes.

5. Meanwhile, arrange the cod fillets on a shallow baking tray and sprinkle over the Cajun spice mix, salt and pepper.

6. Rub the spice mix down into the cod fillets, then brush on the oil using a pastry brush.

7. After the potatoes have been in the oven for 20 minutes, turn them over, using a spatula, and place them back in the oven.

8. Place the cod fillet tray in the oven on a rail above the potatoes and cook for 10–12 minutes, until the cod is cooked through, and the potato wedges are golden.

9. I like to serve the fish and potatoes alongside a simple green salad.

TIP Swap out the cod for any chunky white fish, such as pollock, hake or haddock. It also works well with salmon.

Hunter's chicken

Chicken breast, wrapped in bacon, smothered in tangy barbecue sauce and topped with melted cheese. A British pub classic that you can easily make at home for a quick weeknight dinner.

4 chicken breasts

8 rashers (strips) streaky bacon (smoked or unsmoked – whatever you prefer)

240ml (1 cup) BBQ sauce (good-quality store-bought is fine)

50g (½ cup) grated mature (sharp) Cheddar

50g (½ cup) grated mozzarella

to serve

mashed potato or chips (fries)

vegetables, such as carrots, green beans or broccoli

1. Preheat the oven to 200°C/ 400°F/gas mark 7.

2. Wrap each chicken breast with two rashers of bacon and place in a shallow baking dish.

3. Transfer to the oven and cook for 25 minutes – until the chicken is cooked through and no longer pink in the middle.

4. Remove from the oven and spoon the BBQ sauce on and around the chicken.

5. Sprinkle over the Cheddar and mozzarella.

6. Return the chicken to the oven for 5 minutes, until the cheese has melted.

7. Serve the chicken with mashed potato and vegetables.

TIP If you're using shop-bought BBQ sauce, you can pep it up with a little honey, smoked paprika and/or chilli powder for a sweet, smoky or spicy version.

Quick & easy

19

Creamy chicken Dijon

I love the flavours and textures in this dish. We've got the comforting warmth of the cream and Dijon mustard with the crispy saltiness of the bacon, the lovely buttery-ness of the fresh kale and the crunch of those crumbled pecans. Each bite is a little bit different!

4 chicken breasts
¼ teaspoon salt
¼ teaspoon ground black pepper
¼ teaspoon paprika
1 tablespoon sunflower oil
4 rashers (strips) streaky bacon
1 onion, peeled and chopped
2 garlic cloves, peeled and minced
2 tablespoons Dijon mustard
240ml (1 cup) chicken stock
120ml (½ cup) double
   (heavy) cream
60g (approx. 1 cup) kale,
   finely shredded
50g (½ cup) grated Parmesan
10-12 pecans, roughly chopped
   or crumbled

to serve
boiled new potatoes, sprinkled
   with fresh herbs

1. Place the chicken breasts on a chopping (cutting) board and use a rolling pin to flatten them slightly – so they're about 2cm/¾in thick.
2. Season the chicken breasts with the salt, pepper and paprika and set aside.
3. Heat the sunflower oil in a large frying pan (skillet) over a medium heat and cook the bacon, turning once, until crispy. This should take about 5 minutes.
4. Remove the bacon from the pan, then slice into small pieces.
5. Place the frying pan over a medium-high heat and fry the chicken in the leftover bacon fat until golden on one side (4–5 minutes), then turn the chicken over and move to one side of the pan.
6. Add the onion and garlic to the space in the pan and cook for 3–4 minutes, stirring often, until the onion starts to soften.
7. Stir in the Dijon mustard, then pour in the stock and cream and stir again.
8. Move the chicken back into the centre of the pan and coat in the sauce.

9. Bring the sauce to the boil, then add the kale and simmer gently for 10 minutes, until the chicken is cooked through, and the sauce has thickened.
10. Stir in the Parmesan, then turn off the heat.
11. Scatter over the chopped bacon and pecans.
12. I like to serve mine with boiled new potatoes, sprinkled with some fresh chopped herbs.

TIP I sometimes like to swap out the kale for spinach (but add this only for the final 2 minutes of cooking), or alternatively, top with a big handful of fresh pea shoots just before serving.

Quick & easy

20

Easy chicken curry

A quick and simple mild chicken curry recipe with bags of flavour.
Ready in 30 minutes, it makes a great go-to mid-week meal for the whole family.
It's also freezer-friendly, so you can make a big batch and save some for later.

2 tablespoons sunflower oil

3 chicken breasts (about
  600g/1⅓lb), chopped into
  bite-size chunks

1 large onion, peeled and
  finely chopped

2 garlic cloves, peeled and minced

2 teaspoons minced ginger

2 tablespoons mild curry powder
  (go hotter if you prefer)

1 tablespoon ground coriander

½ tablespoon ground cumin

1 teaspoon paprika

½ teaspoon ground cinnamon

½ teaspoon salt

½ teaspoon ground black pepper

2 tablespoons tomato purée
  (paste)

1 x 400g (14oz) can finely
  chopped tomatoes

240ml (1 cup) chicken stock

1 x 400ml (14oz) can coconut milk

1 tablespoon cornflour
  (cornstarch) mixed with
  2 tablespoons cold water to
  make a slurry (optional)

60g (2 packed cups) baby spinach

to serve
cooked rice
fresh coriander (cilantro)
chilli (red pepper) flakes

1. Heat the oil in a large frying pan
(skillet) over a medium-high heat.
2. Add the chicken and cook for
5 minutes, turning occasionally,
until sealed.
3. Add the onion to the pan
with the chicken and cook for
5 minutes, stirring often, to soften.
4. Add the garlic, ginger, curry
powder, coriander, cumin, paprika,
cinnamon, salt and pepper. Stir
and cook for a further minute.
5. Add the tomato purée, canned
tomato, stock and coconut milk.
Bring to a gentle bubble, then
simmer gently for 10 minutes,
stirring occasionally, until the
chicken is cooked through.
6. If you would like to thicken the
curry, stir in the cornflour slurry.
This is optional, you can leave it
out if the curry thickness is to
your liking.
7. Stir in the spinach (it should wilt
quickly), then turn off the heat.
8. Serve with cooked rice, topped
with fresh coriander and chilli
flakes.

MAKE AHEAD This is a
great curry to make ahead and
it reheats really well. Make the
curry, then quickly cool, cover
and refrigerate or freeze. If
freezing, defrost overnight in the
refrigerator. Reheat in a pan over
a medium heat (you may need to
add a splash of water to loosen it
up) until the chicken is piping hot
throughout.

MAKE IT VEGETARIAN Swap
the chicken for tofu, Quorn or
chunks of courgette (zucchini).
You'll also need to swap the
chicken stock for vegetable stock.

Quick & easy

Chicken fajitas

There's nothing like a bit of Tex-Mex for a quick weekend dinner. This is marinated chicken, seared to perfection, and served with smoky charred peppers and onions.

3 chicken breasts (about 600g/1⅓lb), sliced into strips
3 tablespoons sunflower oil
2 tablespoons fajita seasoning (you can buy this ready-made from the supermarket)
8 small flour tortillas
1 red (bell) pepper, deseeded and sliced
1 green (bell) pepper, deseeded and sliced
1 yellow (bell) pepper, deseeded and sliced
1 onion, peeled and thinly sliced

to serve
1 avocado, sliced (brush with a little lemon/lime juice to prevent browning)
a bunch of fresh coriander (cilantro), roughly chopped
120ml (½ cup) sour cream
250g (1 cup) tomato salsa
50g (½ cup) grated Cheddar
1–2 jalapeños, sliced
1–2 limes, sliced or cut into wedges

1. Preheat the oven to its lowest temperature and place a large baking tray (sheet) in there to warm.
2. Place the chicken on a plate, drizzle over 2 tablespoons of the oil and sprinkle with the fajita seasoning. Rub in until thoroughly coated.
3. Heat a cast-iron griddle (grill) pan to a high heat. When hot, place the tortillas on the griddle, turning once, until you have griddle lines on both sides of the tortillas. It should only take a minute or two, but you'll probably need to do this in two or three batches. Transfer to a plate and cover to keep warm.
4. Brush the griddle with the remaining 1 tablespoon oil.
5. Place the sliced pepper and onion on the griddle and fry until slightly charred and softened (about 8–10 minutes), turning once or twice during cooking.
6. When cooked, transfer the pepper and onion to the warm baking tray in the oven.

7. Place the chicken on the hot griddle and cook until charred and no longer pink in the middle (about 5–6 minutes). Turn over once during cooking.
8. When cooked, serve the chicken with the onion and pepper in the warmed tortillas, garnished with avocado slices and coriander.
9. Place the sour cream, salsa, grated cheese, jalapeños and lime wedges in little bowls, so everyone can add their favourite toppings to their fajitas.

TIP Make extra and save some for a fajita salad bowl the next day. A drizzle of sour cream and a few salad leaves makes a fantastic salad!

Quick & easy

Quick & easy chicken ramen

A quick chicken ramen that uses instant noodles and cooked, shredded chicken for a speedy soup with a flavourful broth. It's delicious and you can make it in 20 minutes!

1 teaspoon sesame oil

2 tablespoons unsalted butter

4 garlic cloves, peeled and minced

2 teaspoons minced ginger

1.4 litres (approx. 6 cups) chicken stock (water plus 4 stock cubes is fine)

2 tablespoons light soy sauce

2 tablespoons dark soy sauce

1–2 tablespoons sriracha hot sauce (depending on how hot you like it)

1 tablespoon Chinese rice wine or sherry

1 tablespoon light brown sugar

¼ teaspoon ground white pepper

3 cooked chicken breasts, shredded (about 340g/12oz)

210g (3 x 70g/2½oz packets) instant noodles (noodles only)

toppings

5 spring onions (scallions), chopped

4 boiled eggs, sliced in half (see Tip)

1 carrot, peeled and julienned

1 teaspoon black and white sesame seeds

2 teaspoons chilli oil or chilli paste, such as sambel oelek

1. Heat the oil and butter in a large saucepan over a medium heat, until the butter melts.

2. Add the garlic and ginger, and fry for 1 minute, stirring often to ensure the garlic doesn't burn.

3. Add the stock, light and dark soy sauce, sriracha, rice wine (or sherry), brown sugar and white pepper.

4. Stir together, then add in the cooked, shredded chicken breast.

5. Turn the heat up to high and bring to the boil, then simmer for 3 minutes to heat through the cooked chicken breast.

6. Add the instant noodles, bring back to the boil, then simmer for 3 minutes, stirring a couple of times to separate the noodles.

7. Use a set of tongs to divide the noodles among four bowls.

8. Ladle over the broth and add the chicken.

9. Top each bowl with spring onion, egg (two pieces each) and carrot.

10. Sprinkle over the sesame seeds and drizzle with a little chilli oil or chilli paste before serving.

TIP To make slightly jammy boiled eggs, place 4 medium eggs in a pan and (just) cover with cold water. Bring to the boil and simmer for 6 minutes. Remove from the pan and place in a bowl of ice water for a couple of minutes, then peel and slice in half.

MAKE AHEAD Make a batch of the broth ahead (without the noodles and chicken). Then you can cool and refrigerate for up to 2 days. Reheat in the pan until boiling, then continue on with the recipe, adding the chicken and noodles.

Quick chicken stir-fry

You don't need to buy ready-made stir-fry sauce to get a stir-fry on the table quickly. Combining a few different ingredients can give you a quick, tasty sauce with a lovely sweet-sour-spicy flavour.

3 chicken breasts (about 600g/1⅓lb), sliced into bite-size pieces

2 tablespoons cornflour (cornstarch)

a pinch of salt and pepper

2 tablespoons sunflower oil

20 sugar snap peas (snow peas)

1 yellow (bell) pepper, deseeded and sliced

1 red (bell) pepper, deseeded and sliced

2 garlic cloves, peeled and minced

4 tablespoons soy sauce

2 tablespoons Chinese rice vinegar

3 tablespoons brown sugar

3 tablespoons sweet chilli sauce

2 tablespoons tomato ketchup

a bunch of spring onions (scallions), chopped

1 small red chilli, deseeded and sliced

to serve

cooked rice or noodles

chopped spring onions (scallions)

1. Place the chicken in a bowl, add the cornflour, salt and pepper and toss together to coat.

2. Add the oil to a wok over a high heat. When the oil is very hot, add the chicken and fry for 5-6 minutes, turning a couple of times until lightly browned.

3. Add in the sugar snap peas and peppers and fry for a further 2 minutes.

4. Add in the garlic, soy sauce, Chinese rice vinegar, brown sugar, sweet chilli sauce and tomato ketchup, toss everything with a spatula and continue to cook over a high heat until heated through.

5. Check the chicken is cooked by taking a large piece and slicing it in half. If it's no longer pink in the middle, it's cooked.

6. Stir through the chopped spring onion and chilli; heat for one more minute until they're hot, but still crunchy.

7. Serve with rice or noodles, topped with a sprinkling of fresh chopped spring onion.

TIP Try adding pineapple chunks and juice from a can, along with a tablespoon each of malt vinegar and sugar and an extra squirt of ketchup for a quick sweet and sour stir-fry.

Quick & easy

29

Teriyaki beef noodles

Juicy strips of steak, stir fried with vibrant vegetables, egg noodles and an easy homemade teriyaki sauce. This noodle dish is packed full of flavour. Comfort food in a bowl!

marinade

2 tablespoons light soy sauce
3 tablespoons dark soy sauce
1 tablespoon sake or dry sherry
3 tablespoons mirin
1 teaspoon sesame oil
1 tablespoon brown sugar
2 teaspoons minced ginger
3 garlic cloves, peeled and minced
½ teaspoon white pepper

stir-fry

500g (1lb 2oz) Denver, sirloin
  (porterhouse) or skirt/flank
  steak, cut into strips (cut
  against the grain)
200g (7oz) medium egg
  noodles (dried)
1 teaspoon sesame oil
1½ tablespoons sunflower oil
1 small onion, peeled and
  finely sliced
1 red (bell) pepper, deseeded
  and thinly sliced
1 carrot, peeled and
  chopped into matchsticks
5 spring onions (scallions),
  sliced into thin strips

to serve

¼ teaspoon chilli (red pepper)
  flakes
1 tablespoon sesame seeds

1. In a bowl, mix together all of the marinade ingredients.

2. Place the sliced beef in a second bowl and add one-third of the marinade. Stir together, cover and leave to marinate for 30 minutes. Reserve the rest of the sauce for later.

3. Meanwhile, cook the egg noodles according to the packet instructions (usually boil for 5 minutes), then drain in a colander and rinse in cold water until completely cold. Toss together with the sesame oil and leave in the colander until needed.

4. Heat 1 tablespoon of the sunflower oil in a wok over a high heat.

5. Using a slotted spoon, lift the steak slices out of the marinade and fry in the hot wok in two batches, for about 2–3 minutes, until just cooked.

6. Transfer the cooked beef to a bowl.

7. Add the remaining ½ tablespoon sunflower oil to the wok and fry the onion, red pepper and carrot for 2–3 minutes, until just starting to soften.

8. Add the reserved marinade/ sauce and bring to the boil.

9. Add the noodles and cook, tossing with tongs, for 2–3 minutes until heated through.

10. Add the beef and spring onion and cook for a further 1-2 minutes, to heat the beef back through.

11. Divide among bowls and top with chilli flakes and sesame seeds before serving.

TIP Make teriyaki chicken noodles by replacing the beef with strips of chicken. You will need to cook the chicken for a few minutes longer to ensure it is fully cooked through and no longer pink in the middle.

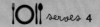
Beef & broccoli

Tender beef steak, stir-fried with broccoli and a heavenly Chinese-style stir-fry sauce. Simple, quick and delicious! It's all ready in 20 minutes so it makes a great mid-week meal for the family.

3 tablespoons sunflower oil

500g (1lb 2oz) skirt/flank steak, sliced very thinly against the grain (see Tip)

300g (10½oz) tenderstem broccoli (broccolini), any thicker pieces sliced in half lengthways

1 teaspoon minced ginger

2 garlic cloves, peeled and minced

sauce

250ml (1 cup + 2 teaspoons) hot beef stock

3 tablespoons light soy sauce

1 tablespoon dark soy sauce

1 tablespoon Chinese rice wine (swap with sherry if you like)

2 teaspoons sesame oil

3 tablespoons light brown sugar

⅛ teaspoon ground white pepper

⅛ teaspoon ground black pepper

2 tablespoons cornflour (cornstarch), mixed with 5 tablespoons cold water to make a slurry

to serve

cooked rice

sesame seeds

1. Start by mixing together all the sauce ingredients EXCEPT the cornflour slurry in a bowl, then set aside.

2. Heat 2 tablespoons of the oil in a wok or large frying pan (skillet) over a high heat.

3. Add the sliced steak and cook for 2–3 minutes, turning once or twice, until the steak is just cooked.

4. Using a slotted spoon, transfer the steak to a bowl, leaving any oil behind in the wok.

5. Add the broccoli to the wok and stir-fry for 2–3 minutes, stirring often, then transfer to the bowl with the steak.

6. Turn the heat down to medium, add the remaining tablespoon of oil and fry the ginger and garlic for 30 seconds, stirring often to ensure it doesn't burn.

7. Add in the sauce mixture, turn the heat up to high and stir together.

8. Allow the sauce to come to the boil, then slowly pour in the cornflour slurry, whilst stirring, until the sauce thickens. You may not need all of the slurry.

9. Add the beef and broccoli back into the wok and toss together. Cook for a further minute, then turn off the heat.

10. Serve with cooked rice and sprinkle with sesame seeds, if you like.

TIP I like to use beef skirt or flank as it's a fairly inexpensive cut of meat with good flavour. It does have to be cut thinly though. If it's cut too thick, it will be chewy. If you prefer, you can use sirloin (porterhouse) or rib-eye steak. These cuts are more tender (and more expensive) so they can be cut a little thicker, if you prefer.

Quick & easy

Chorizo & bean tortilla pan

This easy lasagne-style one-pan meal is made with a smoky chorizo in a bean and vegetable sauce. It's layered up with flour tortillas and my 5-minute white sauce and finished with melted cheese. Serve with fresh coriander (cilantro), sliced red chilli, avocado and sliced red onion.

chorizo sauce

- 1½ tablespoons sunflower oil
- 1 onion, peeled and finely diced
- 1 carrot, peeled and finely diced
- 100g (3½oz) chorizo, chopped
- 2 garlic cloves, peeled and minced
- 1 red or yellow (bell) pepper, chopped into small chunks
- 1 small courgette (zucchini), chopped into small chunks
- 1 teaspoon ground cumin
- 1 teaspoon ground coriander
- ½ teaspoon cinnamon
- ½ teaspoon chilli (red pepper) flakes
- 2 x 400g (14oz) cans chopped tomatoes
- 1 x 400g (14oz) can mixed beans in chilli or tomato sauce
- ¼ teaspoon salt
- ¼ teaspoon ground black pepper

cheese sauce

- 50g (½ cup) grated Cheddar
- 4 tablespoons double (heavy) cream
- 3 tablespoons sour cream
- a pinch of salt and pepper

- 2 large flour tortillas
- 100g (1 cup) mixed Cheddar and Red Leicester cheese, grated

1. Heat the oil in a large frying pan (skillet) over a medium heat. Ensure you use a pan that can also go under the grill (broiler).

2. Add the onion and carrot and cook for 5 minutes, until the onion starts to soften.

3. Add the chorizo and fry for 3–4 minutes, until the chorizo starts to release its oils.

4. Add the garlic, yellow/red pepper and courgette, stir and cook for 2 minutes.

5. Add the cumin, coriander, cinnamon and chilli flakes, stir and cook for 1 minute.

6. Stir in the canned tomato, mixed beans, salt and pepper, bring to a bubble and simmer for 10 minutes.

7. Meanwhile, make the cheese sauce. In a bowl, mix together the cheese, both creams, salt and pepper – you should have a thick, spreadable consistency.

9. Now it's time to assemble the tortilla pan. Spoon out half the chorizo-vegetable sauce into a bowl.

10. Spread out the remaining sauce in the pan to evenly cover the base, then lay one tortilla on top.

11. Spread half of the cheese sauce on top of the tortilla and top with the remaining chorizo-vegetable sauce from the bowl.

12. Place the second tortilla on top, then spread over the remaining cheese sauce and sprinkle with the mixed cheeses.

13. Place the pan over a medium-high heat for a minute, until the sauce starts to bubble at the edges.

14. Turn off the heat and place the pan under a grill (broiler) for 2–3 minutes, until the cheese is melted and bubbling.

15. Remove from the grill and top with fresh coriander, sliced chilli, avocado, red onion and a sprinkling of black pepper.

MAKE IT VEGETARIAN

You can make this vegetarian by swapping the chorizo for 200g (7oz) canned chickpeas that have been drained, rinsed and then mixed with 1 teaspoon smoked paprika. Use vegetarian cheese too.

Quick & easy

34

Pasta dinners.

Hands up if you're a total carb addict like me! I think I could eat pasta every day of the week and never get bored. If you're looking for pasta inspiration, I've got plenty of recipes in this section to up your pasta game, from **Spicy sausage rigatoni** in a lovely warming chilli, tomato and basil sauce to my **Cheesy pasta bake with chicken & bacon**, which is one of the reader favourites on our website. If you're looking for a super-quick recipe, try my **Ravioli in creamy tomato sauce**. It uses shop-bought ravioli, which is given a massive upgrade with my creamy, spicy tomato sauce with lots of lovely sun-dried tomatoes and spinach. Best of all, it's ready in 20 minutes!

Ravioli in creamy tomato sauce

Upgrade that store-bought ravioli to something you'd get at a restaurant with this rich and creamy tomato ravioli sauce with spinach and Parmesan.
You can get it on the table in 20 minutes, and best of all, you can make it all in one pan.

1 tablespoon olive oil

1 onion, peeled and finely diced

2 garlic cloves, peeled and minced

500g (1lb 2oz) fresh ravioli (use your favourite kind)

1 red (bell) pepper, sliced

½ teaspoon Italian herb mix

½ teaspoon chilli (red pepper) flakes

½ teaspoon ground black pepper

a pinch of salt

1 tablespoon tomato purée (paste)

90ml (⅓ cup) white wine

100g (3½oz) roasted or sun-blushed cherry tomato halves (you can buy these from the deli counter)

120ml (½ cup) chicken stock

90ml (⅓ cup) double (heavy) cream

90g (3 packed cups) baby spinach

50g (½ cup) grated Parmesan

1 tablespoon finely chopped flat-leaf parsley

1. Add the olive oil to a large frying pan (skillet) over a medium heat and cook the onion for 4–5 minutes, until it starts to soften.

2. Add the garlic and cook for a further 30 seconds, stirring continuously.

3. Now add the ravioli and red pepper and cook for another minute, stirring a few times.

4. Add the Italian herbs, chilli flakes, black pepper and a pinch of salt, give it a stir then add the tomato purée and wine. Stir again and cook for another minute to reduce the wine slightly.

5. Add the roasted tomatoes, chicken stock and cream, stir everything together and bring up to a simmer. Allow to simmer for 5–6 minutes, until the centre of the ravioli is piping hot (you can open one up to check this).

6. Add the spinach and Parmesan and cook for a minute to allow the cheese to melt and the spinach to wilt.

7. Sprinkle with fresh parsley and serve.

TIP Don't want to use wine? Replace the wine with more chicken stock plus a teaspoon of lemon juice.

MAKE IT VEGETARIAN Use vegetarian ravioli and replace the Parmesan with vegetarian Italian-style hard cheese.

Vegetable pasta bake

This pasta bake is tasty, filling comfort food – a veggie-packed dinner that even the meat-eaters will devour.

400g (14oz) dried pasta shapes

1 tablespoon sunflower oil

1 large red onion, peeled and
chopped into wedges

1 red (bell) pepper, deseeded and
chopped into large chunks

1 yellow (bell) pepper, deseeded
and chopped into large chunks

1 large courgette (zucchini),
chopped into chunks

¼ teaspoon salt

¼ teaspoon ground black pepper

2 garlic cloves, peeled and minced

1 tablespoon tomato purée
(paste)

½ teaspoon dried oregano

½ teaspoon dried thyme

2 x 400g (2 x 14oz) cans chopped
tomatoes

120ml (½ cup) double (heavy)
cream

90g (3 packed cups) fresh
baby spinach

100g (1 cup) grated mature
(sharp) Cheddar

100g (1 cup) grated mozzarella

a small bunch of flat-leaf parsley,
roughly torn, to serve

1. Preheat the oven to 190°C/375°F/gas mark 6.

2. Bring a large pan of salted water to the boil and cook the pasta for 1 minute less than the recommended cooking time on the packet, then drain.

3. While the pasta is cooking, heat the oil in a large frying pan over a medium heat. Add the red onion and cook for 3–4 minutes, until it starts to soften.

4. Add the peppers, courgette, salt, pepper, garlic, tomato purée, oregano and thyme. Stir and cook for 2–3 minutes.

5. Stir in the canned tomato and cream, bring to a gentle bubble, then add the cooked pasta and spinach. Stir everything together, then transfer to a large baking dish.

6. Top with the Cheddar and mozzarella and place in the oven for 20–25 minutes, until the cheese is golden brown.

7. Take out of the oven and scatter with fresh parsley before serving.

MAKE AHEAD You can make this ahead, up to the point where you have sprinkled the cheese on top, then cool, cover with foil and refrigerate for up to a day. Take out of the fridge for an hour before baking it, to take the chill off the dish. Keep the foil on and heat in the oven at 190°C/375°F/gas mark 6 for about 10 minutes, then remove the foil and continue to heat for a further 15 minutes, until hot throughout. But note: the dish will be a little less saucy if you make it ahead, as the pasta will absorb more of the liquid. To ensure it doesn't dry out, you can add a few tablespoons of stock or hot water to the dish before reheating in the oven.

Pasta dinners

Roasted vegetable pesto pasta

*Cherry tomatoes, roasted with garlic, onion, courgette and peppers,
then tossed together with pasta, pesto and cream – this is an easy, meat-free meal,
where the oven does most of the work for you.*

300g (10½oz) cherry tomatoes, sliced in half

2 teaspoons cornflour (cornstarch)

½ teaspoon salt

½ teaspoon ground black pepper

½ teaspoon paprika

2 garlic cloves, peeled

1 red onion, peeled and chopped into bite-size chunks

1 courgette (zucchini), chopped into bite-size chunks

1 red (bell) pepper, sliced

1 yellow (bell) pepper, sliced

2 tablespoons olive oil

400g (14oz) pasta shapes, such as spiralli

3 tablespoons pesto

4 tablespoons double (heavy) cream

to serve

a small bunch of basil leaves

2 tablespoons grated Parmesan

1 tablespoon toasted pine nuts

1. Preheat the oven to 200°C/ 400°F/gas mark 7.

2. Place the tomatoes in a large roasting dish, sprinkle over the cornflour, salt, pepper and paprika and toss together until the tomatoes absorb the cornflour.

3. Add the garlic, red onion, courgette and peppers to the roasting dish. Drizzle over the olive oil and toss together to coat thoroughly.

4. Place in the oven and roast for 20–25 minutes, until golden brown.

5. Meanwhile, cook the pasta as per the packet instructions. Once cooked, drain the pasta using a colander.

6. When the vegetables are golden, remove from the oven and stir in the pesto and cream, then return to the oven for a final 2 minutes, to heat through.

7. Remove the roasting dish from the oven, add the pasta and toss to coat in the sauce.

8. Divide the pasta among bowls and serve topped with fresh basil leaves, grated Parmesan and toasted pine nuts.

TIP Why are we coating the tomatoes in cornflour? As the vegetables roast in the oven, they release liquid. The addition of the cornflour ensures that, as the liquid is released, it's transformed into a thick sauce, which when mixed with the cream and pesto, will be full of flavour.

MAKE IT VEGETARIAN

The pesto and Parmesan in this dish mean that, although it's meat-free, it's not vegetarian. You can easily make it vegetarian by using vegetarian pesto instead of regular pesto, and vegetarian Italian-style hard cheese instead of Parmesan.

Pasta dinners

43

Creamy tuna pasta bake

Canned tuna with pasta, peas and sweetcorn in a lovely creamy, cheesy sauce – this is made with mainly store-cupboard ingredients and is an easy meal that everyone loves!

400g (14oz) pasta

3 tablespoons unsalted butter

1 onion, peeled and finely chopped

40g (⅓ cup) plain (all-purpose) flour

600ml (2½ cups) milk

250g (2½ cups) grated mature (sharp) Cheddar

¼ teaspoon salt

¼ teaspoon ground black pepper

320g (11oz) canned tuna, drained and flaked

330g (11½oz) canned sweetcorn, drained

150g (1 cup) frozen petits pois

½ teaspoon dried parsley or 2 tablespoons chopped flat-leaf parsley, to serve

1. Heat the oven to 180°C/350°F/ gas mark 6.

2. Bring a large pan of salted water to the boil and cook the pasta for 10 minutes.

3. Whilst the pasta is cooking, melt the butter in a saucepan over a low heat and cook the onion for 6–8 minutes, until very soft.

4. Turn the heat up to medium, stir in the flour and, continuously stirring, cook for 1 minute.

5. Slowly add the milk, using a whisk to incorporate (just stir, don't whisk).

6. Continue to heat whilst stirring, until the sauce thickens, then add two-thirds of the cheese and stir until melted.

7. Season with salt and pepper.

8. Drain the pasta and tip into a 20 x 30cm (8 x 12in) baking dish. Pour over the white sauce, then add the tuna, sweetcorn and petits pois. Mix together and sprinkle over the remaining cheese.

9. Bake in the oven for 15–20 minutes, until the cheese is golden brown. Scatter with parsley before serving.

TIP I would always suggest using tuna fish in oil (drain it before adding to the dish) as it has more flavour and a richer texture. However, you can use tuna in water or brine, if you prefer.

MAKE AHEAD Make the dish up to where you sprinkle over the cheese (but don't bake in the oven). Cover and refrigerate for up to 2 days. Take out of the refrigerator an hour before you want to cook it, to take the chill off the dish (and to help prevent cold spots upon heating). Cover with foil and cook in a preheated (190°C/375°F/gas mark 6) oven for 10 minutes, then uncover and cook for a further 20–25 minutes. Check that it's piping hot in the middle before serving.

Pasta dinners

Tomato salmon pasta

This is my way of making three salmon fillets stretch to feed four people.
Plus it's another easy weeknight dinner that can be on the table in 20 minutes!

400g (14oz) rigatoni (or your
 favourite pasta shape)
2 tablespoons olive oil
3 skin-on salmon fillets (approx.
 400g/14oz)
¼ teaspoon salt
¼ teaspoon ground black pepper
1 onion, peeled and
 finely diced
2 garlic cloves, peeled and minced
500g (1lb 2oz) passata
1 tablespoon tomato purée
 (paste)
½ teaspoon dried thyme
1 teaspoon sugar
3 tablespoons double (heavy)
 cream

to serve
grated Parmesan
ground black pepper
basil

1. Cook the pasta as per the packet instructions, then drain, reserving 1 cup of the cooking water.

2. Meanwhile, heat the oil in a large frying pan (skillet) over a medium–high heat.

3. Season the salmon fillets with salt and pepper, then place in the pan skin-side up.

4. Fry the salmon for 3 minutes, until golden, then turn the salmon over and move it to one side of the pan.

5. Add the onion to the space left in the pan and cook over a medium heat for 3–4 minutes, stirring occasionally, until softened.

6. Stir in the garlic and cook for a further 30 seconds.

7. Add the passata, tomato purée, dried thyme and sugar. Stir together and allow to simmer for 2–3 minutes.

8. Turn the salmon over in the frying pan and, using a set of tongs, remove the skin and discard.

9. Using the back of a fork, break up the salmon into chunky pieces.

10. Stir the cream into the sauce.

11. Add the cooked pasta to the pan, along with a good splash (about ¼ cup) of the cooking water.

12. Stir the pasta into the sauce, distributing the pieces of salmon amongst the pasta.

13. Add more of the pasta cooking water if you want to loosen the sauce further.

14. Divide the pasta among bowls and top with a little grated Parmesan, black pepper and a sprinkling of fresh basil leaves.

TIP Add a pinch of chilli (red pepper) flakes for a bit of heat.

Cajun one-pot chicken pasta

This easy Cajun chicken pasta one-pot is a winner for the family dinner table.
There are plenty of colourful veggies and it's ready in 35 minutes!

1 tablespoon sunflower oil

1 onion, peeled and chopped

1½ tablespoons Cajun seasoning

2 chicken breasts (about
  400g/14oz), cut into
  bite-size pieces

75g (2½oz) chorizo, cut into
  small chunks

2 garlic cloves, peeled and minced

½ red (bell) pepper, deseeded
  and sliced

½ green (bell) pepper, deseeded
  and sliced

½ yellow (bell) pepper, deseeded
  and sliced

200g (7 oz) dried pasta shapes
  (I use rigatoni)

400g (14oz) can chopped
  tomatoes

480ml (2 cups) chicken stock

80ml (⅓ cup) double (heavy)
  cream

a large handful of baby spinach

10 cherry tomatoes, sliced in half

50g (½ cup) grated Cheddar

chopped flat-leaf parsley,
  to serve

1. Heat the oil in a large frying pan (skillet) over a medium heat and cook the onion for 5 minutes, stirring occasionally, until it begins to soften.

2. Sprinkle the Cajun seasoning over the chicken, then add to the pan with the onion and cook for 5–6 minutes, until sealed on all sides.

3. Add the chorizo and garlic and fry for a further 2 minutes, until the chorizo starts to release its oils, then add the peppers.

4. Stir together, then add the pasta shapes, canned tomato and chicken stock. Bring to the boil, stir and cover with a lid or some foil.

5. Turn the heat down and let the pasta simmer for 15 minutes. Check and stir once or twice during this time.

6. After 15 minutes, remove the lid and test the pasta. It should be just cooked (if it isn't, cook for a couple of minutes more with a splash of boiling water, if needed).

7. Stir in the cream, heat through for a minute, then turn off the heat and stir in the spinach. It should wilt very quickly.

8. Sprinkle over the sliced tomato, grated cheese and fresh parsley, then serve.

TIP Mushrooms, kale, sun-dried tomatoes and spring onions (scallions) make great additions or swaps for the vegetables in this recipe.

MAKE IT VEGETARIAN

Replace the chicken with tofu or Quorn, or you could even roast some butternut squash or sweet potato and add that instead. Replace the chicken stock with vegetable stock. Leave the chorizo out, or you can replace with vegetarian chorizo or regular vegetarian sausage. If I'm leaving the chorizo out or replacing it with vegetarian sausage, I like to add in a teaspoon of smoked paprika with the Cajun spice so I still get that hint of smoky sweetness.

Pasta dinners

30 minute
one-pot chicken pasta

This one-pot cheesy chicken pasta meal is easy, quick and delicious.
All cooked in one pan and ready in 30 minutes. A brilliant weeknight dinner!

1 tablespoon sunflower oil

1 large onion, peeled and chopped

2 chicken breasts (about
400g/14oz), cut into chunks

a pinch of salt and pepper

2 garlic cloves, peeled and minced

1 tablespoon tomato purée
(paste)

1 red (bell) pepper, deseeded
and chopped

300g (10½oz) dried pasta
shapes, such as spiralli

1 teaspoon dried oregano

½ tablespoon Worcestershire
sauce

2 x 400g (2 x 14oz) cans chopped
tomatoes

300ml (1¼ cups) chicken stock

120ml (½ cup) milk

20 sugar snap peas (snow peas),
roughly chopped

100g (1 cup) grated
mature (sharp) Cheddar

1 tablespoon chopped
flat-leaf parsley

1. Heat the oil in a large frying pan (skillet) over a medium–high heat and cook the onion for 3 minutes, until it starts to soften.

2. Add the chicken, season with salt and pepper and cook for a further 3 minutes, until the chicken is sealed (it won't be cooked in the middle at this point).

3. Add the garlic, tomato purée and red pepper, stir and then add the dry pasta.

4. Now add the oregano, Worcestershire sauce, canned tomato, stock and milk.

5. Stir, bring to the boil, then turn down to a gentle simmer. Cover with a lid or some foil and simmer for 12–15 minutes (checking and stirring occasionally), until the pasta is cooked.

6. Stir in the sugar snap peas (it's nice to add them at the end, so they're hot, but retain their crunch).

7. Sprinkle the pasta with cheese and put it under the grill (broiler) for a couple of minutes until the cheese has melted.

8. Scatter with fresh parsley and serve.

TIP Sprinkle over a little grated mozzarella, as well as the Cheddar, for a stretchy cheese finish.

Pasta dinners

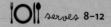
Cheesy pasta bake with chicken & bacon

This cheesy pasta bake is a family favourite. I like to make a big dish of it, as it makes great leftovers too (hot or cold). I love it served up with a big green salad.

400g (14oz) dried pasta shapes (I use rigatoni)

1 tablespoon sunflower oil

3 chicken breasts (about 600g/1⅓lb), cut into bite-size chunks

1 large onion, peeled and chopped

1 red (bell) pepper, deseeded and chopped

1 yellow (bell) pepper, deseeded and chopped

a pinch of salt and pepper

2 garlic cloves, peeled and minced

1 tablespoon tomato purée (paste)

½ teaspoon dried oregano

½ teaspoon dried thyme

2 x 400g (2 x 14oz) cans chopped tomatoes

120ml (½ cup) double (heavy) cream

100g (3 packed cups) baby spinach

6 rashers (strips) cooked bacon, chopped

100g (1 cup) grated mature (sharp) Cheddar

100g (1 packed cup) grated mozzarella

a small bunch of flat-leaf parsley, roughly torn, to serve

1. Preheat the oven to 190°C/ 375°F/gas mark 6.

2. Bring a large pan of water to the boil and cook the pasta for 1 minute less than the recommended cooking time on the packet. Drain.

3. While the pasta is cooking, heat the oil in a large frying pan (skillet) over a medium heat and cook the chicken for about 5 minutes, until just sealed.

4. Add the onion and cook for a further 3–4 minutes, until softened.

5. Add the peppers, salt, pepper, garlic, tomato purée, oregano and thyme.
Stir and cook for 2–3 minutes.

6. Stir in the canned tomato and cream, bring to a gentle bubble, then add the pasta, spinach and cooked bacon. Stir everything together, then transfer to a large baking dish.

7. Top with the Cheddar and mozzarella and place in the oven for 20–25 minutes, until the cheese is golden brown.

8. Take out of the oven and scatter with fresh parsley before serving.

MAKE IT VEGETARIAN

Replace the chicken with chunky pieces of courgette (zucchini) or mushroom. You can leave the bacon out entirely or replace it with vegetarian chorizo or smoky chickpeas (chickpeas fried with smoked paprika, cumin, salt and pepper). Also, ensure the Cheddar and mozzarella are vegetarian versions.

LEFTOVERS Quickly cool, cover and refrigerate any leftovers. You can serve them cold as part of a salad, or reheat in the microwave, in individual portions, for about 2–3 minutes, until piping hot throughout.

Pasta dinners

53

Buffalo chicken pasta

Cajun spiced chicken with pasta and peppers in a tangy, creamy hot pepper sauce. This is an easy 20-minute dinner, packed with loads of flavour. Beware, it's on the hot side!

300g (10½oz) pasta shapes, such as penne

1 tablespoon sunflower oil

3 chicken breasts (about 600g/1⅓lb), chopped into bite-size pieces

1 tablespoon Cajun spice mix

½ teaspoon ground black pepper

1 chicken stock cube, crumbled

2 garlic cloves, peeled and minced

1 onion, peeled and sliced

1 red (bell) pepper, sliced

1 yellow (bell) pepper, sliced

2 jalapeños, sliced

a small bunch of spring onions (scallions), roughly chopped

60ml (¼ cup) hot pepper sauce

1 tablespoon Worcestershire sauce

1 tablespoon cider vinegar

120ml (½ cup) double (heavy) cream

50g (½ cup) grated Parmesan cheese

to serve
sliced jalapeños
sliced spring onions (scallions)

1. Cook the pasta as per the packet instructions. Once cooked, drain, reserving 1 cup of the pasta cooking water.

2. While the pasta is cooking, heat the oil in a large frying pan (skillet) over a medium-high heat.

3. Add the chicken and sprinkle over the Cajun spice and black pepper.

4. Stir to coat the chicken and cook for 5 minutes, stirring occasionally, until the chicken is sealed and nearly cooked through.

5. Sprinkle over the crumbled stock cube and stir together.

6. Add the garlic, onion, peppers and sliced jalapeños and cook for 3–4 minutes, stirring often, until the onion softens slightly.

7. Add the spring onion, hot sauce, Worcestershire sauce, cider vinegar, cream and Parmesan cheese, stir together and bring to a simmer.

8. Simmer for 3–4 minutes, until the chicken is cooked through.

9. Add the pasta to the pan with the chicken and toss to coat.

10. Add in splashes of the pasta cooking water to loosen the sauce a little, if you like.

11. Divide the pasta among bowls and top with sliced jalapeño and spring onion before serving.

TIP I sometimes like to use half the amount of Parmesan and, just before serving, sprinkle over crumbled Lancashire or aged Cheddar. Trust me, those little nuggets of cheese with that spicy chicken are amazing! If you're a fan of blue cheese, then crumbled Stilton is a great (and more traditional) option too.

Pasta dinners

Lasagne

A delicious homemade lasagne with a rich beef ragù, creamy béchamel sauce and golden cheese topping, served with fresh parsley; a comfort food classic.

ragù

1 tablespoon olive oil

1 onion, peeled and finely diced

2 garlic cloves, peeled and minced

1 carrot, peeled and finely diced

3 chestnut (cremini) mushrooms, finely diced

500g (1lb 2oz) minced (ground) beef, 12-20% fat (don't go for the really lean stuff, it's too dry)

3 tablespoons tomato purée (paste)

1 teaspoon dried oregano

½ teaspoon dried thyme

1 tablespoon Worcestershire sauce

1 beef stock cube, crumbled

2 x 400g (2 x 14oz) cans chopped tomatoes

½ tablespoon light brown sugar

½ teaspoon salt

½ teaspoon ground black pepper

béchamel sauce

60g (4 tablespoons) butter (salted or unsalted is fine)

4 tablespoons plain (all-purpose) flour

720ml (3 cups) milk

a pinch of salt and pepper

100g (1 cup) grated Cheddar

12 sheets of dried lasagne

175 g (1¾cups) mixed grated cheese (I use a combination of regular Cheddar, Red Leicester, and mozzarella)

Ragù

1. Heat the oil in a frying pan (skillet) over a medium–high heat and cook the onion for 5 minutes, stirring often, until it softens.

2. Add the garlic and cook for a further minute.

3. Add the carrot and mushroom and cook for a further 2–3 minutes.

4. Add the minced beef and cook for 5–6 minutes, until browned. Stir often, breaking up any large chunks with a spatula.

5. Add the tomato purée, oregano, thyme, Worcestershire sauce, beef stock cube, canned tomato, brown sugar, salt and pepper. Stir and bring to the boil, then turn down the heat and simmer for 15–20 minutes, until thickened.

Béchamel sauce

1. Meanwhile, preheat your oven to 200°C/400°F/gas mark 7 and start on the béchamel sauce.

2. In a medium-size saucepan, melt the butter over a medium heat.

3. Once the butter is melted and bubbling slightly, whisk in the flour and keep gently whisking over the heat for 1–2 minutes, to cook the flour.

4. Add a good splash of milk, turn up the heat and whisk until incorporated.

5. Keep adding the milk, a good splash at a time, stirring with the whisk until all the milk is used up (this normally takes me 3–4 minutes and I add the milk in about 5 splashes). Don't worry if you get a few lumps, keep stirring with the whisk and they will disappear as the sauce thickens.

6. When the sauce has thickened sufficiently, add the salt and pepper and cheese. Stir together, then turn off the heat.

Constructing the lasagne

You'll need a large, fairly deep lasagne dish (I use a rectangular enamel roaster, approx. 30 x 21 x 5cm [12 x 8 x 2in]).

1. Spoon 2 heaped tablespoons of the ragù into the lasagne dish and spread it across the base. You don't need much – this is just to ensure the lasagne sheets don't stick to the bottom of your dish.

2. Cover with four lasagne sheets. Try to ensure they don't overlap. You may need to break up a sheet to cover the dish fully.

3. Spoon on a third of the béchamel sauce and spread it around to cover the lasagne sheets.

4. Cover with a third of the remaining ragù.

5. Place a layer of lasagne sheets on top, followed by a layer of béchamel sauce and ragù. Repeat one more time, until all of the sauce and lasagne sheets are used up.

6. Sprinkle the mixed cheeses on top.

7. Place in the oven and bake for 30 minutes until the cheese is golden and the lasagne is bubbling slightly at the edges.

8. Take out of the oven and leave to rest for 5 minutes before sprinkling with parsley and serving.

MAKE AHEAD Make the lasagne and bake it for 20 minutes, until the cheese is lightly browned. Then cool, cover and refrigerate for up to 2 days. Take out of the refrigerator an hour before you want to bake it – to allow it to come up to room temperature (this helps to avoid cold spots in the middle when you reheat). Place in the oven, covered in foil, for 20–25 minutes at 200°C/400°F/gas mark 7, until piping hot throughout.

Pasta dinners

57

Spaghetti bolognese

My go-to for a rich and satisfying weeknight dinner is often good old spag bol – a classic!
Simple ingredients, without skimping on taste, and it only takes 30 minutes from start to finish.

1 tablespoon olive oil

1 onion, peeled and finely diced

2 garlic cloves, peeled and minced

1 carrot, peeled and finely diced

3 chestnut (cremini) mushrooms, finely diced

450g (1lb) minced (ground) beef

120ml (½ cup) red wine

3 tablespoons tomato purée (paste)

1 teaspoon dried oregano

½ teaspoon dried thyme

1 tablespoon Worcestershire sauce

1 beef stock cube, crumbled

2 x 400g (2 x 14oz) cans chopped tomatoes

½ tablespoon light brown sugar

½ teaspoon salt

½ teaspoon ground black pepper

300g (10½ oz) dried spaghetti (or use fresh pasta)

to serve

a small bunch of spring onions (scallions), chopped

grated Parmesan

1. Heat the oil in a frying pan (skillet) over a medium-high heat and cook the onion for 5 minutes, stirring often, until it softens.

2. Add the garlic and cook for a further minute.

3. Add the carrot and mushroom and cook for a further 2–3 minutes.

4. Add the minced beef and cook for 5–6 minutes, until browned. Stir often, breaking up any large chunks with a spatula.

5. Add the wine, bring to the boil and let it bubble for 2–3 minutes, until reduced by three-quarters.

6. Add the tomato purée, oregano, thyme, Worcestershire sauce, beef stock cube, canned tomato, brown sugar, salt and pepper. Stir and bring to the boil, then turn down the heat and simmer for 15–20 minutes, until thickened.

7. Meanwhile, bring a large pan of salted water to the boil. Add the spaghetti and cook for 10–12 minutes, until al dente.

8. Drain the spaghetti and divide among bowls.

9. Spoon the bolognese on top of the spaghetti and sprinkle over the spring onion and Parmesan before serving.

TIP The wine adds a little extra richness to the dish. You can leave it out if you prefer, or you could replace with 120ml (½ cup) beef stock and an extra splash of Worcestershire sauce.

MAKE AHEAD The bolognese sauce can be made ahead, then cooled, covered and refrigerated or frozen. Defrost overnight in the refrigerator. Reheat in a pan until piping hot throughout. I like to make a double batch of the bolognese, then serve half and freeze half for a later meal.

Four cheese mac 'n' cheese with bacon

Why have one type of cheese, when you can have four!
This oozy, stretchy, ultra-cheesy mac 'n' cheese is so warming, rich and tasty.
Don't forget that all-important sprinkling of crispy bacon at the end!

200g (7oz) spiral pasta

60g (4 tablespoons) unsalted butter

60g (½ cup) plain (all-purpose) flour

480ml (2 cups) milk

75g (¾ cup) grated mature (sharp) Cheddar

75g (¾ cup) grated Gouda

75g (¾ cup) grated mozzarella

50g (½ cup) grated Parmesan

6 rashers (strips) lightly grilled bacon, roughly chopped

½ teaspoon salt

½ teaspoon ground black pepper

2 tablespoons chopped flat-leaf parsley

1. Preheat the oven to 200°C/400°F/gas mark 7.

2. Cook the pasta in salted boiling water for 1 minute less than the recommended cooking time, then drain.

3. While the pasta is cooking, melt the butter in a medium-size saucepan over a medium heat.

4. Once the butter is melted and bubbling slightly, whisk in the flour and keep gently whisking over the heat for 1–2 minutes, to cook the flour.

5. Add in a good splash of milk, turn up the heat and whisk until incorporated.

6. Keep adding the milk, a good splash at a time, stirring with the whisk until all the milk is used up (this normally takes me 3–4 minutes and I add the milk in about five splashes). Don't worry if you get a few lumps, keep stirring with the whisk and they will disappear as the sauce thickens.

7. When the sauce has thickened sufficiently, add the salt and pepper and cheese, reserving 1 heaped tablespoon of each type of cheese. Stir together, then turn off the heat.

8. Add the cooked and drained pasta to the pan with the sauce. Mix together until the sauce coats the pasta.

9. Transfer the pasta to a baking dish and sprinkle over the reserved cheese and lightly cooked bacon.

10. Bake in the oven for 15–20 minutes, until golden brown.

11. Scatter over fresh parsley and serve.

TIP You don't have to use spiral pasta; use your favourite pasta shape.

Spicy sausage rigatoni

Tomato, chilli, basil and crumbled sausage make a mouthwatering combination;
Punchy flavours that all work together SO WELL. Using sausages instead of
minced (ground) pork or beef adds extra flavour – due to the seasoning in the sausages.
You can also change up the recipe when you want a change
by using different kinds of sausages, see Tip.

300g (10½oz) dried rigatoni pasta

2 tablespoons olive oil

1 small onion, peeled and
   finely diced

1 red (bell) pepper, finely chopped

2 garlic cloves, peeled and minced

1 red or green chilli, finely
   chopped

400g (14oz) good-quality pork
   sausages

2 tablespoons tomato purée
   (paste)

¼ teaspoon ground black pepper

½ teaspoon chilli (red pepper)
   flakes

1 teaspoon dried oregano

1 x 400g (14oz) can finely
   chopped tomatoes

¼ teaspoon salt (optional –
   depending on the saltiness of
   your sausages)

60ml (¼ cup) double (heavy)
   cream

a small bunch of basil,
   sliced into strips

to serve
grated Parmesan

1. Cook the pasta as per the packet instructions, then drain, reserving 1 cup of the pasta water.

2. While the pasta is cooking, heat the olive oil in a large frying pan (skillet) over a medium-high heat.

3. Add the onion, red pepper, garlic and chilli, and cook, stirring often, for 5 minutes, until the onion starts to soften.

4. Remove the skins from the sausages, then add the sausage meat to the pan. Fry for 5–6 minutes, breaking up the sausage meat with a wooden spoon, until browned.

5. Add the tomato purée, pepper, chilli flakes and oregano and stir together, then add the canned tomato. Bring to the boil and simmer for 5 minutes.

6. Taste the sauce and check for seasoning (you may not need any, depending on how heavily seasoned the sausages are).

7. Add the cooked pasta, cream and half the basil and stir together to combine. If you want to loosen the sauce, add in splashes of the reserved cooking water, whilst stirring.

8. Heat for a further 1–2 minutes, to warm through the cream, then turn off the heat.

9. Serve topped with the rest of the fresh basil and some grated Parmesan.

TIP Try different sausage flavours to make this dish different every time! Spicy sausages, herby sausages and chicken sausages are great options.

MAKE IT VEGETARIAN
Use vegetarian sausages and replace the Parmesan with vegetarian Italian-style hard cheese.

Fake-away favourites.

I love a takeaway from our local Chinese as much as anyone – especially when everyone wants a different dish for dinner. But there's nothing quite like making your own fake-away version. A fake-away doesn't have to mean making it extra healthy, it's just about learning how to cook those favourites yourself and modifying them to suit your own tastes. Sometimes I want bacon in my **Egg-fried rice**, sometimes I want chillies in my **Sweet & sour chicken** and sometimes I want a ridiculous amount of sauce to pour over my **Mushroom chow mein**. That's the beauty of making it yourself.

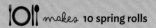

Vegetable spring rolls

Crispy spring rolls, filled with a seriously flavourful vegetarian filling.
I love to serve them with a lots of sweet chilli sauce for dipping.

1 tablespoon sunflower oil

1 tablespoon sesame oil

2 carrots, peeled and sliced
    into matchsticks

140g (5oz) green or white
    cabbage, thinly sliced

½ red (bell) pepper, deseeded
    and thinly sliced

140g (5oz) beansprouts

2 garlic cloves, peeled and minced

4 tablespoons light soy sauce

2 tablespoons hoisin sauce

¼ teaspoon white pepper

2 teaspoons cornflour
    (cornstarch) mixed with
    2 tablespoons cold water to
    make a slurry

oil, for deep frying

10 spring roll pastry wrappers

to serve

sweet chilli sauce

1. Start by making the filling. Heat the sunflower oil and sesame oil in a frying pan (skillet) or wok over a medium-high heat.

2. Add the carrot, cabbage and red pepper and stir-fry for 1 minute, until slightly softened.

3. Add the beansprouts and garlic and toss together, cooking for 1 minute.

4. Add the soy sauce, hoisin sauce and white pepper and toss together, then add in tiny splashes of the cornflour slurry, until the vegetable mixture is slightly sticky (you may not need all of it).

5. Turn off the heat and transfer the vegetables to a plate to cool.

6. Heat the frying oil in a heavy-based pan while you make up the spring rolls.

7. Take a spring roll wrapper and place on the work surface with a corner pointing toward you (cover the rest of the wrappers with a damp tea [dish] towel to stop them from drying out).

8. Place a heaped tablespoon of the cooled vegetable mix near the bottom corner of the spring roll wrapper, leaving about 2½cm/1in of space from the bottom corner, and shape the filling into a sausage shape (the filling will be horizontal to you).

9. Roll up the spring roll, tucking the outer edges in just before you finish rolling – so you have a fat cigar-shaped spring roll. Seal the edges, using a splash of cold water on your fingers.

10. Place the filled spring roll on a plate, then repeat with the remaining spring rolls.

11. When the spring rolls are complete, and your oil is hot, carefully add five spring rolls to the pan, one at a time. You will need to work in two batches to prevent overcrowding the pan.

12. Cook the spring rolls for 2–3 minutes, turning often until golden brown, then transfer to a plate lined with kitchen paper, to soak up any excess oil.

13. Repeat with the remaining spring rolls.

14. Serve with sweet chilli sauce for dipping.

TIP If you want a meat version, you can add thin strips of cooked pork, chicken or duck to the pan, when you add the beansprouts.

Fake-away favourites

Mushroom chow mein

I'm using chestnut mushrooms for this chow mein but you can use your favourite variety and don't be shy with them! You might think 400g mushrooms looks like a lot, but they cook down, so I usually end up throwing extra in.

200g (7 oz) dried chow mein noodles

3 tablespoons sunflower oil

400g (14oz) chestnut (cremini) mushrooms, sliced

¼ teaspoon salt

½ teaspoon ground black pepper

1 onion, peeled and sliced

2 garlic cloves, peeled and minced

1 large carrot, peeled and sliced into matchsticks

1 red (bell) pepper, deseeded and sliced

½ savoy cabbage, thinly sliced

200g (7oz) beansprouts

10 spring onions (scallions), cut into 5cm (2in) lengths

chow mein sauce

1 tablespoon cornflour (cornstarch)

2 tablespoons dark soy sauce

1 tablespoon Chinese rice wine

2 tablespoons kecap manis (sweet soy sauce)

2 tablespoons hoisin sauce

90ml (⅓ cup) vegetable stock

1 tablespoon sesame oil

¼ teaspoon white pepper

to serve

2 spring onions (scallions), roughly chopped

1 teaspoon sesame seeds

¼ teaspoon chilli (red pepper) flakes

1. Start by making the sauce. In a small bowl, mix together the cornflour, soy sauce and Chinese rice wine, until the cornflour is fully incorporated.

2. Add the kecap manis, hoisin sauce, vegetable stock, sesame oil and white pepper. Mix together to combine, then set side.

3. Boil the chow mein noodles as per the packet instructions, then drain and run under cold water to stop them sticking together.

4. Heat the oil in a wok over a high heat. Add the mushrooms, season with salt and pepper and stir-fry for 3 minutes, until the mushrooms are soft.

5. Add the onion, garlic and carrot, and stir-fry for a further 3 minutes, regularly tossing everything together with a spatula.

6. Add the red pepper, cabbage, beansprouts and spring onion and fry again for 2 minutes, keeping everything moving in the wok with your spatula.

7. Add the noodles and pour over the chow mein sauce.

8. Stir-fry everything together for 2–3 minutes, tossing regularly with a set of tongs, until the noodles are hot.

9. Serve topped with spring onion, sesame seeds and chilli flakes.

TIP Swap out the vegetables for whatever you like. Sugar snap peas (snow peas), sliced green beans, courgetti (zoodles) all work great.

Fake-away favourites

Egg-fried rice

*A quick recipe for takeaway-style egg-fried rice with loads of flavour!
As tempting as it is to skimp on the oil, I'd advise against it – the oil helps to
ensure separate, flavourful, evenly fried grains of tasty rice.*

2 tablespoons sunflower oil

1 onion, peeled and diced

2 garlic cloves, peeled and minced

800g (4 cups) boiled and cooled long-grain rice (this is about 300g (1½ cups) dried rice that has been boiled in water)

½ tablespoon sesame oil

2 eggs

2 tablespoons dark soy sauce

¼ teaspoon salt

¼ teaspoon garlic salt

1 tablespoon lemon juice (fresh or bottled is fine)

to serve

½ bunch of spring onions (scallions), chopped

1. Heat 1 tablespoon of the oil in a large wok over a medium heat and cook the onion, stirring regularly, for 5 minutes until it softens and turns translucent.

2. Add the remaining sunflower oil and garlic and cook for 30 seconds, stirring regularly.

3. Add the rice, turn the heat up to high and drizzle over the sesame oil.

4. Use a spatula to toss everything together and ensure the rice doesn't stick to the bottom of the pan. Keep moving the rice around so that it's all getting reheated.

5. Once the rice is hot (this will take about 5 minutes), push the rice over to the side of the pan and crack the eggs into the space. Add a little splash (about ¼ tablespoon) of the soy sauce to the eggs.

6. Making sure the part of the wok with the eggs in is over the heat, fry the eggs, giving a mix with the spatula until the egg starts to cook and look scrambled, but is still a little runny.

7. Now mix the egg into the rice.

8. Pour in the remaining soy sauce, sprinkle over the salt and garlic salt and mix it all together.

9. Add the lemon juice, stir and taste, adding a little more if required.

10. Divide among 4 bowls and top with spring onion.

TIP Be sure to use cooked cold rice, rather than warm rice. Rice dries a little as it cools, and this dryness will help stop the fried rice going sticky and claggy. Rice that has cooled and dried a little will also absorb more flavour.

Fake-away favourites

70

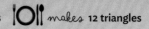

Sesame prawn toast

Making this crispy prawn toast at home means you can modify it to your own taste (which for me means LOTS of prawns!). Top slices of bread with a simple whizzed-up prawn (shrimp) mixture, coat in sesame seeds and fry to golden perfection. You can have these ready in less than 20 minutes!

200g (7oz) raw prawns (shrimp), shelled and deveined

1 teaspoon minced ginger

2 garlic cloves, peeled and minced

1 egg white

2 spring onions (scallions), finely chopped

1 teaspoon light soy sauce

¼ teaspoon salt

¼ teaspoon ground white pepper

3 pieces of thick sliced white bread

6 tablespoons sesame seeds

sunflower oil for frying, around 1 litre (4¼ cups)

to serve

1 tablespoon chopped fresh coriander (cilantro)

2 tablespoons sweet chilli sauce

1. Add the raw prawns, ginger, garlic, egg white, spring onion, light soy sauce, salt and white pepper to a mini food processor and blitz until you have a paste.

2. Slice the bread (no need to remove the crusts) with two diagonal cuts across each piece from corner to corner, leaving you with four triangles of bread for each slice (so 12 triangles altogether).

3. Spread the prawn paste evenly across one side of each bread triangle. It should be roughly 1 tablespoon of paste for each triangle.

4. Place the sesame seeds onto a plate or in a shallow bowl.

5. Dip each of the triangles, paste-side down, into the sesame seeds so you get a nice even covering of sesame seeds on the paste, then transfer to a plate, ready for frying.

6. Heat the oil in a wok or deep frying pan over a high heat, until it's hot but not smoking (test by placing a small chunk of bread into the oil; if it floats and starts to sizzle then the oil is hot enough).

7. Working in two or three batches (see Tip), lay the triangles in the oil, paste-side down, and cook for 1–2 minutes, then turn them over and cook for 30–60 seconds, until the bread is golden, and the prawn paste is cooked through.

8. Transfer to a plate or tray lined with kitchen paper to soak up any excess fat.

9. Repeat until all of the prawn toasts are cooked.

10. Sprinkle over some fresh coriander and serve with the sweet chilli sauce.

TIP Be sure to cook in batches. If you overcrowd the pan, this will reduce the temperature of the oil, which, in turn, means the prawn toast will take longer to cook and the bread will soak up more oil, resulting in greasy oily prawn toast, which nobody wants!

MAKE AHEAD These are best made and served right away. If the uncooked paste is left on the bread for too long, the bread may go soggy. However, you can make the prawn mixture 3-4 hours in advance, then cover and refrigerate it. Then you can make up the prawn toast right before cooking.

Crispy sesame chicken

This crispy coated chicken in a sweet, sticky and slightly spicy sauce is the most popular recipe on our website. It's one of my family's favourites too – it doesn't last 5 minutes on the dinner table!

5 tablespoons sunflower oil

2 eggs, lightly beaten

3 tablespoons cornflour (cornstarch)

75g (⅔ cup) plain (all-purpose) flour

½ teaspoon salt

½ teaspoon ground black pepper

½ teaspoon garlic salt

2 teaspoons paprika

3 chicken breasts (about 600g/1lb 5oz), chopped into bite-size chunks

sauce

1 tablespoon sesame oil

2 garlic cloves, peeled and minced

1 tablespoon Chinese rice vinegar (white wine vinegar will work too)

2 tablespoons honey

2 tablespoons sweet chilli sauce

3 tablespoons ketchup

2 tablespoons brown sugar

4 tablespoons soy sauce

to serve

cooked rice

2 tablespoons sesame seeds

a small bunch of spring onions (scallions), chopped

1. Heat the oil in a wok or large frying pan (skillet) until very hot.

2. Whilst the oil is heating, place the egg in a shallow bowl and the cornflour in another shallow bowl. Add the flour, salt, pepper, garlic salt and paprika to another shallow bowl and mix together.

3. Dredge the chicken in the cornflour, then dip in the egg (make sure all of the chicken is covered in egg wash), and finally dredge it in the seasoned flour.

4. Working in two batches, add the chicken to the wok and cook over a high heat for 6–7 minutes, turning two to three times. When well browned, transfer to a bowl lined with kitchen paper.

5. Add all of the sauce ingredients to the hot wok, stir and bubble over a high heat until the sauce reduces by about a third (it should take 2–3 minutes).

6. Add the chicken back to the wok and toss in the sauce to coat. Cook for 1–2 minutes.

7. Turn off the heat and divide among four bowls. Serve with cooked rice and top with sesame seeds and spring onion.

TIP This recipe makes enough sauce to coat the chicken. If you like lots of sauce (enough to drizzle over your rice), double the sauce ingredients.

Sweet & sour chicken

Who can argue with crispy coated fried chunks of chicken in a lip-smackingly tangy sauce, which is made mostly from store-cupboard ingredients? Serve with plenty of boiled or fried rice to soak up that sauce!

chicken

5 tablespoons sunflower oil

2 eggs, lightly beaten

3 tablespoons cornflour (cornstarch)

90g (¾ cup) plain (all-purpose) flour

½ teaspoon salt

½ teaspoon ground black pepper

½ teaspoon garlic salt

2 teaspoons paprika

3 chicken breasts (about 600g/1⅓lb), chopped into bite-size chunks

sauce

1 tablespoon sunflower oil

1 large onion, peeled and chopped into large chunks

1 red (bell) pepper, chopped into 2½cm (1in) pieces

1 green (bell) pepper, chopped into 2½cm (1in) pieces

2 garlic cloves, peeled and minced

1 teaspoon minced ginger

150ml (⅔ cup) tomato ketchup

1 tablespoon tomato purée (paste)

2 tablespoons malt vinegar

6 tablespoons dark brown muscovado sugar

475g (17oz) canned pineapple chunks in juice

to serve

Egg-fried rice (see page 70)

1. Heat the oil in a wok or large frying pan (skillet) until very hot.

2. Whilst the oil is heating, place the egg in a shallow bowl and the cornflour in another shallow bowl. Add the flour, salt, pepper, garlic salt and paprika to another shallow bowl and mix together.

3. Dredge the chicken in the cornflour, then dip in the egg (make sure all of the chicken is covered in egg wash), and finally dredge it in the seasoned flour.

4. Working in two batches, add the chicken to the wok and cook over a high heat for 6–7 minutes, turning two or three times. When well browned, transfer to a bowl lined with kitchen paper.

5. Whilst the chicken is cooking, you can start on your sauce.

6. Add the oil to a large frying pan over a medium-high heat and cook the onion for 3 minutes, stirring occasionally, until it turns translucent.

7. Add the peppers and cook for a further minute.

8. Add the garlic and ginger and cook for another minute.

9. Add the tomato ketchup, tomato purée, vinegar, dark brown sugar and the canned pineapple (including the juice) and stir. Bring to the boil, then turn down the heat and let it bubble (stirring every so often) until slightly thickened.

10. Transfer the cooked crispy chicken to the pan with the sauce and toss to coat, cooking for a minute or two, then turn off the heat.

11. Serve with egg-fried rice.

TIP Does the coating ever fall off when you cook coated chicken? If so, it's because the chicken releases steam when it's cooked. If you leave coated chicken too long before adding to a sauce, the steam being released from the chicken can cause the coating to loosen. So try to ensure you cook the chicken immediately before making the sauce.

Fake-away favourites

Salt & pepper chicken

*Crispy seasoned chicken, fried up with crunchy onions and spicy chillies –
this recipe is a real flavour explosion.*

60g (½ cup) cornflour
(cornstarch)

1 tablespoon table salt

1¼ tablespoons ground black
pepper

1 tablespoon Chinese five-spice

6 skinless chicken thigh fillets
(about 540g/1¼lb), quartered

sunflower oil, for frying (around
240ml/1 cup)

1 large onion, peeled and chopped
into large chunks (about
2cm/1in across)

1 red chilli, chopped into small
pieces (I use relatively mild
fresno or serrano chillies)

1 green chilli, chopped into small
pieces

2 garlic cloves, peeled and minced

3 spring onions (scallions),
roughly chopped

1. In a bowl, mix together
the cornflour, ¾ tablespoon of
the salt, 1 tablespoon of the black
pepper and the Chinese five-spice.

2. Sprinkle the mixture over the
chicken thigh fillets and toss
to coat.

3. Place the sunflower oil (minus
1 tablespoon) in a large frying pan
(skillet) over a high heat until hot.
You can test by sticking the end of
a wooden spoon or chopstick in
the oil – if bubbles form around it,
it's hot enough.

4. Add the chicken to the oil one
piece at a time (to ensure the oil
doesn't boil over). You'll probably
have to work in two batches
altogether.

5. Fry the chicken for about
5–7 minutes, turning once, until
cooked through and golden brown
all over.

6. Using a set of tongs, transfer
the chicken to a plate lined with
kitchen paper.

7. Repeat with the second batch
of chicken, then turn off the heat.

8. As soon as the second batch
of chicken is cooking, heat the
reserved 1 tablespoon oil in a
separate large frying pan (skillet)
over a medium-high heat.

9. Add the onion, red and green
chillies, the remaining
¼ tablespoon salt and the
remaining ¼ tablespoon black
pepper to the pan. Fry for about
2–3 minutes, stirring often, until
the onion starts to soften slightly.

10. Turn the heat down to
medium, add the garlic and spring
onion and fry for a further minute,
stirring often.

11. By now, both batches of
chicken should be cooked, so add
the chicken to the frying pan with
the onion and chillies and toss
everything together for a minute.

12. Turn off the heat and serve.

TIP If you want to change the
spice level, swap out the chillies
for (bell) peppers for a non-spicy
finish, or use hotter chillies, such
as Thai chillies, for a hotter finish.

Fake-away favourites

Honey garlic chicken

Sticky tender boneless chicken thighs in a garlic, soy and honey sauce.
It's so simple to make and ready in 20 minutes!
Serve with rice for an easy Friday night fake-away.

8 skinless chicken thigh fillets
(about 720g/1½lb)
2 tablespoons cornflour
(cornstarch)
½ teaspoon salt
½ teaspoon ground black pepper
2 tablespoons sunflower oil
1 tablespoon unsalted butter
4 garlic cloves, peeled and minced
110g (⅓ cup) honey
80ml (⅓ cup) chicken stock
1 tablespoon rice vinegar
1 tablespoon light soy sauce

to serve
1 tablespoon finely chopped
flat-leaf parsley
½ teaspoon chilli (red pepper)
flakes
cooked rice

1. Place the chicken thighs in a bowl and add the cornflour, salt and pepper. Toss together until fully coated.
2. Heat the oil in a large frying pan (skillet) over a high heat.
3. Add the chicken thighs and cook on one side until golden brown (about 4–5 minutes), then turn over and cook for a further 2 minutes.
4. Add the butter to the pan, let it melt, then add the garlic and stir together. Turn the heat down to medium so the garlic doesn't burn, then make the sauce.
5. To make the sauce, combine the honey, stock, rice vinegar and light soy sauce in a bowl and stir together.
6. Add the sauce to the pan. Turn the heat up and bring the sauce to the boil, then simmer for 4–5 minutes until the sauce reduces and thickens and the chicken is cooked through (and no longer pink in the middle).
7. Sprinkle over the chopped parsley and chilli flakes and serve over cooked rice.

TIP If you don't have rice vinegar, you can swap for cider vinegar or white wine vinegar plus ¼ teaspoon sugar.

Fake-away favourites

Crispy duck

This is my easy method for oven-roasted Peking duck with crispy skin and juicy, fall-apart meat. I glaze the duck in plum sauce for the last few minutes in the oven for a beautiful, flavourful skin. It works so well for that classic Chinese restaurant starter with cucumber, spring onion and pancakes. There won't be a shred left!

1 duck (about 2.4kg/5⅓lb), innards removed
½ teaspoon salt
½ teaspoon ground black pepper
2 tablespoons plum sauce

to serve
12 Chinese pancakes, warmed
1 bunch of spring onions (scallions), sliced into thin strips
1 cucumber, sliced into thin strips

1. Preheat the oven to 150°C/300°F/gas mark 3. Take a large roasting tin (pan) and place a wire rack inside.
2. Pat the duck down with kitchen paper to ensure the skin is dry.
3. With a sharp knife, score the skin of the duck in a criss-cross pattern (breast side). Be sure not to pierce the flesh.
4. Place the duck (breast-side up) on the rack in the tin.
5. Season with salt and pepper and place in the oven for 3 hours 30 minutes. Turn the duck over every hour (I use a clean kitchen towel in each hand to turn the duck over).
6. After the duck has cooked for 3 hours 30 minutes, take it out of the oven and turn the oven temperature up to 190°C/375°F/gas mark 6.
7. Turn the duck so that it's breast-side up again and brush with the plum sauce.
8. Place the duck back in the oven for 10 minutes until the glaze has turned dark brown and caramelized.

9. Take the duck out of the oven, leave to rest for 10 minutes, then place on a large plate and shred the meat using two forks.
10. Serve immediately with more plum sauce, pancakes and strips of spring onion and cucumber.

TIP Turning the duck every hour ensures the fat evenly distributes throughout the meat as the duck is cooking (basically, like continually basting the meat). It also helps to ensure that perfect crispy skin.

Black pepper beef

Tender strips of steak, stir-fried in a warming black pepper sauce with peppers and onions. A quick but luxurious dinner!

450g (1lb) thin sirloin (porterhouse) steak, sliced thinly against the grain

¼ teaspoon salt

2 teaspoons ground black pepper

4 tablespoons sunflower oil

1 teaspoon sesame oil

2 onions, peeled and chopped into thick slices

1 green (bell) pepper, deseeded and sliced

1 red (bell) pepper, deseeded and sliced

2 tablespoons cornflour (cornstarch)

2 tablespoons dark soy sauce

2 tablespoons oyster sauce

1 tablespoon Chinese rice wine (or replace with dry sherry)

120ml (½ cup) beef stock

2 garlic cloves, peeled and minced

1 teaspoon minced ginger

to serve
cooked rice

1. Toss the steak slices with the salt and 1 teaspoon of the black pepper.

2. Heat 3 tablespoons of the sunflower oil with the sesame oil in a wok (or large frying pan/skillet) over a high heat until hot, then add the steak.

3. Fry the steak for 2–3 minutes, moving it around the wok so it doesn't stick together, until browned.

4. Using a slotted spoon, transfer the steak to a bowl, leaving any oil behind in the wok. Turn the heat down to medium.

5. Add the remaining 1 tablespoon sunflower oil to the wok and stir-fry the onion and (bell) pepper for 3–4 minutes, until starting to soften.

6. Whilst the vegetables are cooking, place the cornflour, dark soy sauce, oyster sauce and Chinese rice wine in a bowl and stir together until the cornflour is mixed in.

7. Add the beef stock and the remaining 1 teaspoon of black pepper to the sauce. Stir together to combine, then set aside.

8. Coming back to the wok, add the garlic and ginger to the vegetables and cook for 1 minute, stirring often.

9. Pour in the sauce, stir together and let it come to a gentle simmer. If it looks too thick, you can add a splash of water.

10. Add the steak back to the wok and stir through to coat in the sauce. Cook for a further 2 minutes to heat the steak back through.

11. Serve the black pepper beef over cooked rice.

TIP Don't feel like beef? Swap out the beef for thin strips of pork or chicken.

Fake-away favourites

Crispy chilli beef

Perfect crispy strips of beef in a tangy spicy sauce. This is my favourite dish from the Chinese takeaway, so it has a lot to live up to. It's really important to get that lovely craggly exterior on crispy chilli beef. The secret? You need to use cornflour AND egg, and no, you don't need to use the deep-fryer! I like to serve mine sprinkled with fresh red chilli and with rice.

360g (13oz) thin-cut sirloin (porterhouse) steaks (approx. 3 thin steaks), cut into thin strips (see Tip)

1 small egg

4 tablespoons cornflour (cornstarch)

¼ teaspoon salt

¼ teaspoon ground black pepper

⅛ teaspoon white pepper

4½ tablespoons sunflower oil,

1 onion, peeled and sliced into thin strips

1 red chilli, finely sliced (discard the seeds if you don't like it too hot)

1 teaspoon minced ginger

3 garlic cloves, peeled and minced

2 tablespoons rice vinegar

3 tablespoons dark soy sauce

2 tablespoons tomato purée (paste)

6 tablespoons caster (superfine) sugar

2 tablespoons tomato ketchup

2 tablespoons sweet chilli sauce (I use Thai-style)

1. Place the steak strips in a bowl and add the egg. Mix together to coat the steak thoroughly.

2. Add the cornflour, salt and pepper and toss together. It will be a sticky mixture.

3. Heat 3 tablespoons of the oil in a large frying pan (skillet) or wok, over a high heat, until very hot. You can test by sticking the end of a wooden spoon or chopstick in the oil – if bubbles form around it, it's hot enough.

4. Working in two batches, add half the beef, a strip at a time, and spread it out.

5. Fry the steak until dark brown and crispy. Try not to move the meat around too much as this reduces the amount of crispiness you get. It generally takes about 5–6 minutes to crisp up the beef, with about three or four stirs during that time.

6. Using a slotted spoon or tongs, transfer the beef to a plate lined with kitchen paper to soak up any excess fat.

7. Add a further tablespoon of oil and cook the second batch of beef, then transfer to the plate along with the first batch.

8. Add the remaining ½ tablespoon oil to the pan and turn the heat down to medium.

9. Add the onion and cook for 2 minutes, until slightly softened.

10. Add the chilli, ginger and garlic and cook, stirring, for 30 seconds.

11. Add the rice vinegar, soy sauce, tomato purée, sugar, tomato ketchup and sweet chilli sauce to the pan.

12. Turn up the heat and let it bubble for a couple of minutes, until the sauce starts to reduce a little.

13. Return the beef to the wok, give it a stir and heat through for 1–2 minutes, until the beef is hot.

14. Serve with rice or noodles.

TIP It's easier to cut the steak into thin strips if you place it in the freezer for 30 minutes beforehand, to firm up a little.

Sticky Chinese-style pork belly

This Sticky Chinese-style pork belly is one of my absolute favourite recipes on the blog. It uses my three-step process for pork that's meltingly tender, with a crispy exterior and gloriously sticky, sweet and spicy coating.

1kg (2¼lb) rindless pork belly slices

1 litre (4¼ cups) hot chicken or vegetable stock

1 teaspoon minced ginger

3 garlic cloves, peeled and cut in half

1 tablespoon rice wine

1 tablespoon caster (superfine) sugar

glaze

2 tablespoons sunflower oil

a pinch of salt and pepper

1 teaspoon minced ginger

1 red chilli, finely chopped

2 tablespoons honey

2 tablespoons brown sugar

3 tablespoons dark soy sauce

1 teaspoon lemongrass paste

1. Add all the pork belly slices, stock, ginger, garlic, rice wine and sugar to a large casserole pan. I use a cast-iron casserole pan.

2. Bring to the boil, then cover with a lid, turn down the heat and simmer gently for 2 hours.

3. Turn off the heat and drain the pork, reserving the liquid if you like (it's perfect for a Thai or Chinese noodle soup).

4. Using a sharp knife, slice the pork into bite-size chunks.

5. Place the glaze ingredients (minus 1 tablespoon oil) in a small bowl and stir together.

6. Heat the oil in a frying pan (skillet) over a medium-high heat, season the pork and fry, turning occasionally, until it starts to turn golden (about 5 minutes).

7. Pour the glaze over the pork and continue to cook for another 2–3 minutes, until the pork starts to look sticky.

8. Remove from the heat and serve.

TIP Want to use your slow cooker? You can do the first stage of cooking the pork in the broth mixture in the slow cooker. Cook on high for 4–5 hours or low for 6–7 hours.

MAKE AHEAD You can cook the pork in the stock and aromatics ahead of time, then cool, cover and refrigerate (for up to 2 days) or freeze. Defrost in the refrigerator overnight before slicing and frying the meat as per the rest of the recipe. You can also make the sauce ahead, then cover and refrigerate it up to a day ahead.

Curries.

We have a curry at least once a week. It's always the default meal that goes into the menu when I'm planning our food. I've got some super-quick curries – like the **Thai red chicken curry** or the **Prawn balti**, or lovely mild curries – such as the **Chicken korma** and **Butter chicken**. Then there are the slow-cooked, tender curries. I have to recommend the **Beef massaman**, made with fall-apart beef and baby new potatoes. So sumptuous! The **Chicken tikka masala** is a big family favourite – if you have a barbecue, then try it on skewers for a beautiful smoky finish. If you want a real show-stopper to make for your friends, then try the **Chicken biryani** with its delicious, complex flavours.

Creamy paneer curry

*This vegetarian curry uses chunks of creamy paneer in a fragrant butter-style curry sauce.
It's mild enough for the whole family to enjoy, but you can
spice it up with the addition of some fresh chillies, if you like it hotter.*

1 large onion, peeled and
  roughly chopped
4 garlic cloves, peeled
1 thumb-sized piece of ginger,
  peeled and roughly chopped
3 tablespoons unsalted butter
1 tablespoon sunflower oil
¼ teaspoon salt
1½ tablespoons garam masala
1 tablespoon medium-heat
  curry powder
1 teaspoon paprika
½ teaspoon cinnamon
180ml (¾ cup) chicken stock
400g (14oz) passata
2 tablespoons tomato purée
  (paste)
2 teaspoons sugar
6 cardamom pods
175ml (¾ cup) double
  (heavy) cream
450g (1lb) paneer cheese,
  chopped into bite-size chunks

to serve
fresh coriander (cilantro), roughly
  chopped
thinly sliced red onion
nigella seeds
naan

1. Place the onion, garlic and ginger in a food processor and blend until smooth.

2. Heat the butter and oil in a large frying pan (skillet) over a medium-high heat and cook the onion, garlic and ginger for 5–6 minutes, stirring occasionally until the onion starts to brown at the edges of the pan.

3. Add the salt, garam masala, curry powder, paprika and cinnamon. Stir and cook for 1–2 minutes, until the spices start to release their fragrance.

4. Add the stock, passata, tomato purée, sugar and cardamom, bring to the boil and simmer for 10 minutes, until thickened.

5. Remove the cardamom, then stir in the cream and allow to heat through.

6. Carefully stir in the paneer and cook for a further 3 minutes, until the paneer is heated through.

7. Serve with freshly chopped coriander, thinly sliced red onion and a sprinkling of nigella seeds. I like to serve mine with naan for dipping too.

TIP I like to sew cardamom pods together with a piece of natural cotton. This makes it much easier when you want to find them and fish them out later.

Chickpea & sweet potato curry

Ready in 35 minutes, this lightly spiced, fragrant curry with chickpeas, tender chunks of sweet potato and fresh spinach is easy to prepare and packed full of flavour. Great for vegetarians and meat-eaters alike, it's also mild enough for the kids to enjoy, but still packs a flavour punch!

2 tablespoons sunflower oil

1 large onion, finely chopped

2 garlic cloves, minced

2 teaspoons minced ginger

2 tablespoons mild curry powder (go hotter if you prefer)

1 tablespoon ground coriander

½ tablespoon ground cumin

1 teaspoon paprika

½ teaspoon ground cinnamon

½ teaspoon salt

½ teaspoon ground black pepper

2 medium sweet potatoes (around 450g/1lb altogether), peeled and chopped into 2cm/¾in chunks

1 x 400g (14oz) can chickpeas, drained

2 x 400g (2 x 14oz) cans chopped tomatoes

2 tablespoons tomato purée (paste)

1 x 400g (14oz) can coconut milk

60g (2 packed cups) baby spinach

to serve

cooked basmati or pilau rice

fresh coriander (cilantro)

red onion slices

1. Heat the oil in a large frying pan (skillet) over a medium-high heat.

2. Add the onion and cook for 5 minutes, stirring often, to soften.

3. Add the garlic, ginger, curry powder, coriander, cumin, paprika, cinnamon, salt and pepper. Stir and cook for a further minute.

4. Add the sweet potato, chickpeas, canned tomato, tomato purée and coconut milk.

5. Bring to a gentle bubble, then simmer gently, stirring occasionally, for 20–25 minutes – until the sweet potato has softened. If the sweet potato is still firm (this depends on the size of the chunks) you can cook for 5–10 minutes more. Add a splash of water or veggie stock if the sauce starts to look too thick.

6. Stir in the spinach (it should wilt quickly), then turn off the heat.

7. Serve with basmati or pilau rice, topped with fresh coriander and sliced red onion.

TIP Want to cook in the slow cooker? Follow the recipe up until the point you bring the curry to a simmer, then transfer to the slow cooker and cook on high for 3–4 hours, or low for 5–6 hours. Stir in the spinach just before serving.

MAKE AHEAD Make the curry, then cool quickly, cover and refrigerate for up to 2 days. Reheat in a pan, or in the microwave, stirring often, until piping hot throughout.

Prawn balti

A super-quick, medium-spiced tasty curry. When cooked in Indian restaurants, this is usually cooked in single portions in a traditional balti dish. However, I'm cooking it in a larger pan so it can serve four.

2 tablespoons sunflower oil (or ghee)

1 large onion, peeled and chopped into large chunks

1 red (bell) pepper, deseeded and roughly chopped

1 green (bell) pepper, deseeded and roughly chopped

2 garlic cloves, peeled and minced

2 teaspoons minced ginger

1 green chilli, thinly sliced

3 cardamom pods

¼ teaspoon salt

½ teaspoon ground black pepper

1 teaspoon ground cumin

1 teaspoon ground coriander

1 teaspoon turmeric

1 teaspoon paprika

2 teaspoons garam masala

¼ teaspoon ground cinnamon

¼ teaspoon hot chilli powder (add more if you like it hotter)

2 tablespoons tomato purée (paste)

1 x 400g (14oz) can finely chopped tomatoes

120ml (½ cup) chicken stock

2 medium tomatoes, chopped

20-25 raw king (jumbo) prawns (shrimp), shelled and deveined

to serve
cooked rice
chapati
fresh coriander (cilantro)

1. Heat the oil in a large frying pan (skillet) over a medium-high heat.

2. Add the onion and cook for 3 minutes, stirring occasionally, until just starting to soften.

3. Add the peppers, garlic, ginger, chilli and cardamom pods and fry for 2–3 minutes, until just starting to soften.

4. Add the salt, pepper, cumin, coriander, turmeric, paprika, garam masala, cinnamon, chilli powder and tomato purée. Stir together to coat the vegetables.

6. Add the canned tomato, chicken stock and chopped tomatoes, stir together, bring to the boil and simmer for 5 minutes, until slightly reduced.

7. Add the prawns and cook for 3–4 minutes, until the prawns are pink and cooked through.

8. Serve with rice and chapati, topped with fresh coriander.

TIP You can use ready-cooked king (jumbo) prawns, cooking for the same amount of time. Just ensure they're piping hot throughout.

Curries

Monkfish coconut curry

*Living in a beautiful little harbour town with the most fantastic fish available,
I love experimenting with fish recipes. This monkfish curry is fantastic –
the lovely firm flesh of the monkfish works so well with the creamy coconut curry sauce.*

2 tablespoons sunflower oil

1 large onion, peeled and
finely chopped

1 red (bell) pepper, deseeded and
sliced in strips

2 garlic cloves, peeled and minced

2 teaspoons minced ginger

2 tablespoons medium-heat
curry powder

1 tablespoon ground coriander

½ tablespoon ground cumin

1 teaspoon paprika

½ teaspoon salt

½ teaspoon ground black pepper

2 tablespoons tomato purée
(paste)

1 x 400g (14oz) can finely
chopped tomatoes

240ml (1 cup) chicken stock

1 x 400ml (14oz) can coconut milk

500g (1lb 2oz) monkfish fillets,
chopped into meaty chunks

100g (3½oz) extra-fine green
beans, cut in half

1 tablespoon cornflour
(cornstarch) mixed with
2 tablespoons cold water to
make a slurry (optional)

60g (2 packed cups) baby spinach

to serve
cooked rice
fresh coriander (cilantro)
1 red chilli, finely sliced
naan

1. Heat the oil in a large frying pan (skillet) over a medium-high heat.

2. Add the onion to the pan and cook for 5 minutes, stirring often, until softened.

3. Add the pepper, garlic, ginger, curry powder, coriander, cumin, paprika, salt and pepper. Stir and cook for a further 2 minutes.

4. Add the tomato purée, canned tomato, stock and coconut milk. Stir together and bring to a gentle bubble.

5. Add the monkfish chunks and green beans and cook for 6–8 minutes, until the monkfish is cooked through.

6. If you would like to thicken the curry, slowly pour in the cornflour slurry, whilst stirring, until the thickness is to your liking.

7. Stir in the spinach (it should wilt quickly), then turn off the heat.

8. Serve with cooked rice, topped with fresh coriander and slices of fresh chilli, and naan on the side.

TIP Swap out the green beans or add in more veggies, if you like. Peas, chunks of fresh tomato or samphire all work really well with this dish. Just add them in for the last 5 minutes of cooking.

Chicken tikka masala

Tender chunks of marinated, chargrilled (charbroiled) chicken in a creamy mild sauce with garlic, ginger and spices. Serve with cooked rice, flatbreads, coriander (cilantro) and red onion slices.

chicken

3 chicken breasts (about 600g/1⅓lb), chopped into bite-size chunks
120ml (½ cup) Greek yogurt
2 garlic cloves, peeled and minced
1 tablespoon minced ginger
juice of ½ lemon
1 teaspoon ground coriander
½ teaspoon turmeric
½ teaspoon ground cumin
1 teaspoon paprika
½ teaspoon mild chilli powder
a pinch of cinnamon
½ teaspoon salt
½ teaspoon ground black pepper
2 tablespoons sunflower oil

masala sauce

1 tablespoon sunflower oil
1 tablespoon unsalted butter
1 onion, peeled and finely chopped
3 garlic cloves, peeled and minced
2 teaspoons minced ginger
1 teaspoon garam masala
2 teaspoon ground coriander
2 teaspoons paprika
1 teaspoon ground cumin
½ teaspoon cinnamon
2 tablespoons tomato purée (paste)
1 red (bell) pepper, finely chopped
1 x 400g (14oz) can chopped tomatoes
180ml (¾ cup) double (heavy) cream
3 tablespoons ground almonds
1 tablespoon brown sugar

1. Place the chicken breast pieces in a bowl or freezer bag with the yogurt, garlic, ginger, lemon juice, coriander, turmeric, cumin, paprika, chilli powder, cinnamon, salt and pepper. Mix together so that everything is combined, then cover and place in the fridge to marinate for 2–3 hours.

2. About 35–40 minutes before you're ready to eat, start on the sauce.

3. Heat the oil and butter in a large frying pan (skillet) over a medium-high heat until melted. Add the onion and cook for 4–5 minutes, until softened.

4. Add the garlic, ginger, garam masala, coriander, paprika, cumin, cinnamon and tomato purée. Stir and cook for 2–3 minutes, to allow the spices to release their fragrance.

5. Add the pepper, canned tomato and 120ml (½ cup) water. Stir and bring to the boil, then simmer for 15–20 minutes, until thickened.

6. While the sauce is simmering, take the marinated chicken out of the fridge and spread out onto a baking sheet.

7. Brush the chicken with the oil, then grill (broil) for 8–10 minutes, until a little charred on the outside. If your pieces aren't too big, you shouldn't need to turn them, but if they're not cooking through

underneath, then give them a turn with some tongs. Make sure the chicken is cooked by slicing into a larger piece and ensuring it's no longer pink in the middle.

8. When the sauce is ready, stir in the cream, ground almonds and sugar, followed by the cooked chicken tikka. Cook for a further 5 minutes to heat through.

9. Serve with cooked rice and/ or flatbreads and top with fresh coriander. I like to sprinkle over some red onion slices too.

TIP Extra chicken tikka pieces taste great as part of a salad or in a wrap for lunch the next day.

MAKE AHEAD You can make this whole dish ahead. Cool, cover and refrigerate for up to 2 days. Reheat in a pan, covered with a lid, over a medium heat for 10-15 minutes, until piping hot throughout.

Thai red chicken curry

An easy Thai curry, made with chicken, coconut milk and shop-bought red curry paste.
So tasty and aromatic! A great option when you're short on time but don't want to miss out on taste.

1 tablespoon sunflower oil

1 onion, peeled and chopped

3 chicken breasts (about 600g/1⅓lb), chopped into bite-size pieces

2 garlic cloves, peeled and minced

1 teaspoon minced ginger

1 teaspoon lemongrass paste

1 chicken stock cube, crumbled

4 tablespoons red Thai curry paste

1 red (bell) pepper, sliced

1 x 400g (14oz) can coconut milk

2 teaspoons fish sauce

1 tablespoon palm sugar or light brown muscovado sugar

1 x 255g (8oz) can bamboo shoots, drained

10 Thai basil leaves

1 tablespoon lime juice (about ½ lime)

to serve

cooked rice

Thai basil leaves

fresh coriander (cilantro)

Thai chillies, thinly sliced

1 lime, sliced into wedges

1. Heat the oil in a large frying pan (skillet) over a medium-high heat.

2. Add the onion and cook for 3–4 minutes, stirring occasionally, until softened.

3. Add the chicken and cook for 2–3 minutes, until sealed.

4. Add the garlic, ginger, lemongrass paste and crumbled stock cube and stir together to coat the chicken.

5. Add the curry paste, stir and cook for a further 3 minutes, stirring occasionally.

6. Add the (bell) pepper and cook for a minute.

7. Add the coconut milk, fish sauce, palm sugar, bamboo shoots and Thai basil leaves. Bring to the boil, then gently simmer for 10 minutes, until thickened.

8. Stir in the lime juice, then serve the curry with cooked rice.

9. Top with fresh Thai basil leaves, coriander (cilantro), chilli slices and lime wedges before serving.

TIP Go for full-fat coconut milk for the best creamy flavour, without worrying that your sauce might split (as can happen with low-fat coconut milk).

MAKE AHEAD You can make this curry, then cool, cover and refrigerate for up to 2 days. Reheat in a pan until piping hot throughout.

Curries

Thai green chicken curry

*My deliciously rich and aromatic Thai Green Chicken Curry is
made beautifully vibrant and fresh-tasting, due to the homemade curry paste.
Easily made mild or hot, depending on how many chillies you add.*

thai green curry paste

- 3–6 green chillies (depending on how spicy you like it, you could reduce further to 1–2 and remove the seeds for less heat)
- 6 spring onions (scallions), roughly chopped
- 2 teaspoons lemongrass paste
- 1 thumb-size piece of ginger, peeled and roughly chopped
- 4 garlic cloves, peeled and roughly chopped
- 6 kaffir lime leaves
- zest and juice of 1 lime
- ½ teaspoon salt
- ¼ teaspoon white pepper
- ½ tablespoon ground cumin
- 1 tablespoon ground coriander
- 1 teaspoon shrimp paste
- 2 teaspoons fish sauce
- a large bunch of coriander (cilantro), stalks too

chicken curry

- 2 tablespoons sunflower oil
- 4 chicken breasts (about 800g/1¾lb), cut into bite-size chunks
- 4 heaped tablespoons homemade Thai Green Curry Paste (see above)
- 1 chicken stock cube, crumbled
- 1 x 400ml (14oz) can coconut milk
- 1 head of broccoli, broken into small florets
- 150g (1 cup) sugar snap peas (snow peas)
- 1 x 255g (8oz) can bamboo shoots, drained
- 1 teaspoon light brown sugar

to serve

- cooked rice
- Thai basil leaves
- freshly chopped red chillies

1. Start by making the curry paste. In a high-powered blender, place the green chillies, spring onion, lemongrass, ginger, garlic, kaffir limes leaves, lime zest and juice, salt, white pepper, cumin, ground coriander, shrimp paste and fish sauce. Pulse until fully combined.

2. Add the large bunch of fresh coriander (stalks too) and pulse again until smooth. You might need to scrape down the sides a couple of times to ensure it's fully combined. Set aside.

3. Heat the oil in a large frying pan (skillet) over a medium-high heat. Add the chicken and fry for 5–6 minutes, until just cooked through.

4. Add the curry paste you made earlier – you need about 4 heaped tablespoons. Stir and cook through for 2–3 minutes.

5. Sprinkle over the stock cube, stir, then pour in the coconut milk and heat through until the sauce is very hot but not boiling.

6 Add the broccoli, sugar snap peas and bamboo shoots and stir together. Heat through for a few more minutes, stirring often, until the vegetables are lightly cooked, but still crisp.

7. Stir in the sugar.

8. Serve over rice, topped with Thai basil and freshly chopped red chillies.

MAKE AHEAD The veggies won't be quite as crunchy, but this curry can be made ahead and reheated. Cook the curry as per the instructions, then cool quickly, cover and refrigerate for up to a day. Reheat in a pan over a medium heat (don't boil rapidly or it may split) until piping hot throughout.

Butter chicken

This butter chicken is lovely and rich but without the heat of some curries.
It comes with plenty of sauce to soak into the rice and, once the chicken is marinated,
it only takes 30 minutes to pull it all together.

chicken & marinade

4 chicken breasts (about
    800g/1¾lb), diced
80ml (⅓ cup) natural yogurt
1 tablespoon lemon juice
1 garlic clove, peeled and minced
1 teaspoon garam masala
1 teaspoon ground coriander
1 teaspoon paprika
1 teaspoon mild chilli powder

for the sauce

1 onion, peeled and chopped
4 garlic cloves, peeled
2 teaspoons minced ginger
3 tablespoons butter
1 tablespoon sunflower oil
¼ teaspoon salt
1½ tablespoons garam masala
1 tablespoon curry powder
1 teaspoon paprika
½ teaspoon cinnamon
120ml (½ cup) chicken stock
    (or water plus a stock cube)
400g (14oz) passata
2 tablespoons tomato purée
    (paste)
2 teaspoons sugar
6 cardamom pods (see Tip on
    page 92)
175ml (¾ cup) double (heavy)
    cream

to serve

fresh coriander (cilantro)
rice and/or naan

1. Place the chicken in a bowl
with the marinade ingredients, stir
together, cover and refrigerate.
Leave to marinate for a minimum
of 1 hour (or overnight).
2. To make the sauce, place the
onion, garlic and ginger in a food
processor and blend until smooth.
3. Heat the butter and oil in a large
frying pan (skillet) over a medium-
high heat until the butter melts.
4. Add the minced onion, garlic
and ginger to the pan and cook for
5–6 minutes, stirring occasionally,
until the onion starts to brown at
the edges of the pan.
5. Add the marinated chicken and
cook for 3–4 minutes, until sealed.
6. Add the salt, garam masala,
curry powder, paprika and
cinnamon. Stir and cook for
1–2 minutes, until the spices start
to release their fragrance.
7. Add the stock, passata, tomato
purée, sugar and cardamom,
bring to the boil and simmer for 15
minutes.
8. Remove the cardamom, then
stir in the cream and allow to
heat through.
9. Serve sprinkled with some
freshly chopped coriander
alongside some rice
and/or naan.

TIP If you want more of a chicken
tikka butter chicken, you can grill
(broil) the marinated chicken
before adding to the dish.

MAKE AHEAD Make the
curry, then quickly cool, cover
and refrigerate for up to 2 days.
Reheat in a pan over a medium
heat (you may need to add a
splash of water to loosen it up)
until the chicken is piping hot
throughout.

Curries

Chicken korma

This chicken korma is made with coconut cream, yogurt and a small amount of ground almonds. It's rich, creamy and mild, with lots of flavour, so perfect for kids and adults to enjoy. It's all cooked in one pan with no marinating required and it's ready in less than 30 minutes!

2 tablespoons ghee or sunflower oil

1 onion, peeled and finely chopped

3 chicken breasts (about 600g/1⅓lb), chopped into bite-size chunks

2 garlic cloves, peeled and minced

2 teaspoons minced ginger

1 teaspoon ground cumin

1½ teaspoons ground coriander

1½ teaspoons garam masala

½ teaspoon mild chilli powder (optional)

½ teaspoon turmeric

¼ teaspoon salt

¼ teaspoon white pepper

2 tablespoons tomato purée (paste)

120ml (½ cup) natural yogurt

120ml (½ cup) coconut cream (see Tip)

2 tablespoons ground almonds

1 tablespoon sugar

60ml (¼ cup) double (heavy) cream

to serve
cooked rice
naan
freshly chopped coriander (cilantro)

1. Heat the ghee in a large frying pan (skillet) over a medium heat, until hot.

2. Add the onion and cook for 5 minutes, stirring often, until softened.

3. Add the chicken and cook for 5 minutes, stirring occasionally, until the chicken is sealed.

4. Add the garlic, ginger, cumin, ground coriander, garam masala, chilli powder, turmeric, salt, white pepper and tomato purée.

5. Cook for 2 minutes, stirring, until the chicken is coated.

6. Add the yogurt, coconut cream, ground almonds and sugar.

7. Stir everything together, bring to a gentle boil, then simmer for 6–8 minutes, until the chicken is cooked through.

8. Stir in the cream and turn off the heat.

9. Serve the korma with rice and/or naan, topped with fresh coriander (cilantro).

TIP Coconut cream is thicker than coconut milk, with a higher fat content. You can use the little cans of coconut cream or use creamed coconut blocks, mixed with a little hot water to make coconut cream. If you only have coconut milk, you can chill the can overnight, then open the can and use the solid portion at the top of the can, leaving the liquid behind.

MAKE AHEAD You can make this curry ahead, then cool, cover and refrigerate for up to 2 days. Reheat in a pan over a medium heat, stirring often, until the chicken is piping hot throughout. The sauce will have thickened so you may need to add a little water or cream to loosen it when reheating.

Curries

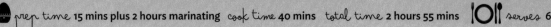
Chicken biryani

Tender chicken in a richly spiced sauce, layered with fragrant, flavour-packed rice and topped with saffron and thinly sliced fried onion. Usually, I prefer Indian dishes with lots of sauce, but there's so much flavour in this dish (and it's anything but dry!) that it's perfect as it is. Don't be put off by the length of this recipe and the number of ingredients. It's actually quite simple, and very calming and relaxing to make, and the results are so worth it.

6 skinless chicken thigh fillets
(about 540g/1¼lb), cut in half

marinade

180ml (¾ cup) natural yogurt
2 tablespoons sunflower oil
4 garlic cloves, peeled and minced
1 tablespoon minced ginger
2 tablespoons tomato purée
(paste)
¼ teaspoon asafoetida (see Tip)
½ teaspoon turmeric
2 teaspoons garam masala
½ teaspoon ground fenugreek
2 teaspoons ground coriander
1 teaspoon ground cumin
¼ teaspoon ground cinnamon
3 cardamom pods
2 teaspoons mild chilli powder
(medium or hot if you like it
really spicy)
2 mild green chillies, roughly
chopped
1¼ teaspoons salt
1 tablespoon lemon juice

par-cooked rice

2 teaspoons salt
5 cloves
1 teaspoon cumin seeds
3 bay leaves
2 cardamom pods
450g (2¼ cups) white
basmati rice

crispy fried onions

4 tablespoons sunflower oil
2 onions, peeled and sliced

3 tablespoons chopped fresh
coriander (cilantro)
1 tablespoon chopped mint
leaves
1 teaspoon saffron threads
3 tablespoons milk
3 tablespoons ghee, melted
(or use unsalted butter)
2 tablespoons toasted flaked
almonds

to serve

natural yogurt
chopped fresh coriander
(cilantro)

1. Place the chicken in a bowl with all of the marinade ingredients.
2. Stir together to coat, then cover and place in the refrigerator for at least 2 hours (or overnight).
3. For the rice, heat 1½ litres (6 cups) water in a saucepan, along with the salt, cloves, cumin seeds, bay leaves and cardamom pods, until boiling.
4. Add the rice, stir once, bring back to the boil and simmer (uncovered) for 5 minutes.
5. Drain the rice in a sieve and set aside.
6. Now make the fried onions. Heat the oil in a deep cast-iron casserole pan over a medium heat.
7. Add the onion and cook for 10–15 minutes, stirring occasionally, until dark brown. Be careful not to burn them, as they will taste bitter. Note – we're going to be using the same cast-iron pan to cook the biryani, so if you're worried the onions are catching on the pan (which may affect the taste of the biryani), you can fry them in a separate frying pan (skillet).
8. Using a slotted spoon, scoop the onion out of the pan (and the oil) and transfer to a bowl for later.

9. Now take the marinated chicken out of the refrigerator and add to the pan with the oil from the onions. Stir in 3 tablespoons water.

10. Cook the chicken over a medium heat for 2–3 minutes, stirring a couple of times, to very lightly seal the chicken.

11. Now scatter the chopped coriander and mint over the chicken.

12. Next, spoon the rice on top of the chicken and flatten it out slightly.

13. Mix together the saffron and milk and let it sit for a minute, then drizzle the mixture over the rice, followed by the melted ghee.

14. Spoon over the fried onions and toasted almonds.

15. Place a lid on the pan, but leave just a tiny gap.

16. As soon as you see steam coming from the gap, place the lid on fully, turn the heat down to low and cook for 20 minutes, then turn off the heat and allow to rest for 10 minutes.

17. Top with a little more fresh coriander, if desired, and serve with extra yogurt.

TIP Asafoetida, also known as hing, is a spice used in some Indian dishes. It adds a deep savoury flavour, like onion or garlic, to a dish. You only need a little (too much is overpowering). If you can't get hold of any, or if you're unlikely to use it for anything else, then don't worry, it can be left out. There are plenty of spices already in the dish to give it a fantastic flavour.

MAKE AHEAD If you want to prep some of the stages ahead, you can marinate the chicken, fry the onions and par-cook the rice in the morning, then put it all together in the evening.

Curries

Beef massaman curry

*This delicious, rich, fall-apart slow-cooked massaman curry is perfect comfort food!
Make extra and freeze some for a busy weeknight.*

massaman paste

1 red onion, peeled and chopped
1–3 mild red chillies, chopped
2 teaspoons ground coriander
2 teaspoons ground cumin
½ teaspoon ground cinnamon
½ teaspoon white pepper
3 garlic cloves, peeled
2 teaspoons lemongrass paste
1 teaspoon minced ginger
1 teaspoon shrimp paste
3 teaspoons fish sauce
1 teaspoon brown sugar
small bunch of fresh coriander
　(cilantro) stalks
½ teaspoon salt

other curry ingredients

1½ tablespoons cornflour
　(cornstarch)
¼ teaspoon salt
¼ teaspoon ground black pepper
1kg (2¼lb) braising beef (beef
　chuck), chopped into chunks
2 tablespoons sunflower oil
400ml (1⅓ cups) beef stock (or
　2 stock cubes with water is fine)
1 x 400g (14oz) can coconut milk
500g (1lb 2oz) baby new potatoes
juice of 1 lime

to serve

cooked rice
sliced red chillies
sliced spring onions (scallions),
fresh coriander leaves
lime wedges

1. Place all of the paste ingredients in a food processor or mini chopper and blend until it forms a paste. Set aside.

2. Place the cornflour, salt and pepper in a bowl and toss the beef to coat.

3. Heat the oil in a large pan over a medium–high heat and fry the meat for about 5 minutes. You can do this in batches but I find that, if you put the meat in and leave it alone for a few minutes before you stir it, you'll get a nice dark colour on the beef. The beef will probably stick a bit to the pan; if so, give it a little scrape with a spatula.

4. Turn down the heat a little and add the spice paste. Stir to coat the beef and let it cook for a couple of minutes.

5. Add the beef stock and coconut milk, give everything a stir (make sure you scrape any bits stuck to the bottom of the pan), bring to the boil, cover with a lid and gently simmer over a low heat for 1 hour 45 minutes. (Alternatively, you can place in the oven at about 160°C/320°F/gas mark 4 for the same amount of time.) Give it a stir every so often. If it's starting to look dry, add in a splash of beef stock or water.

6. After 1 hour 45 minutes, stir in the potatoes and cook for a further 25–30 minutes, until the potatoes are tender (this is a good time to start cooking your rice too).

7. Take off the heat and stir in the lime juice. Serve the curry on a bed of rice with a sprinkling of sliced chillies and spring onion. I also like to serve mine with fresh coriander leaves and lime wedges.

TIP I like to use baby new potatoes in this, but you can use fingerlings or larger potatoes. Ideally, use a waxy potato that will hold together during cooking. Charlotte, Jersey Royals and Yukon Gold all work great – simply wash and chop into chunks (no need to peel).

MAKE AHEAD Once cooked, cool, cover and refrigerate, for up to 2 days, or freeze. Defrost overnight in the refrigerator and reheat in a pan (stirring often) or microwave until piping hot throughout. Add a splash of water or stock to loosen it up if needed.

Curries

113

Beef Madras

This is melt-in-the-mouth beef, slow-cooked in a rich, spicy sauce. The heat also cooks out a little in this recipe, so it's more of a warming heat, rather than a hard-hitting raw heat.

1 large onion, peeled and roughly chopped

3 garlic cloves, peeled

1 thumb-size piece of ginger, peeled and roughly chopped

3 tablespoons sunflower oil or ghee

500g (1lb 2oz) braising beef (beef chuck), cut into bite-size chunks

2 bay leaves

2 tablespoons tomato purée (paste)

½ teaspoon ground cinnamon

3 tablespoons hot Madras curry powder

¼ teaspoon ground fenugreek

½ teaspoon tamarind paste

½ teaspoon salt

½ teaspoon ground black pepper

480ml (2 cups) beef stock

420g (1¾ cups) passata

to serve

cooked basmati rice

naan

fresh coriander (cilantro), roughly chopped

finely sliced red onion

1. Preheat the oven to 160°C/320°F/gas mark 4.

2. Place the onion, garlic and ginger in a food processor and blend to a smooth paste.

3. Heat 2 tablespoons of the oil or ghee in a large casserole pan over a medium-high heat.

4. Add the beef and cook, stirring a couple of times, until browned. This should take 7–8 minutes.

5. Using a slotted spoon, transfer the beef to a plate and set aside.

6. Add the remaining 1 tablespoon of oil to the pan and cook the onion paste, together with the bay leaves, for 5–6 minutes, stirring occasionally, until the onion starts to brown slightly at the edges of the pan.

8. Add in the tomato purée, cinnamon, ton curry powder, fenugreek, tamarind paste, salt and pepper.

7. Stir together and cook for 2–3 minutes, until the spices start to release their fragrance.

8. Add in the beef stock and passata, stir and bring to the boil, then add the beef (plus any resting juices) back to the pan.

9. Cover the pan with a lid and place in the oven for 3 hours, until the beef is tender. Check the beef a couple of times during the last hour of cooking and top up with a splash of boiling water if it's starting to look dry.

10. Once cooked, serve the Madras with basmati rice and/or naan, and top with fresh coriander and red onion slices.

TIP If you want to add some vegetables to this curry, I recommend the addition of mushrooms and/or chopped (bell) peppers. Add them in right before the curry goes into the oven.

MAKE AHEAD This dish can be made ahead, then cooled, covered and refrigerated for up to 2 days. Reheat in a pan, covered with a lid, over a medium heat, for 10-15 minutes, stirring occasionally, until piping hot throughout.

Classics.

There's a good reason why these dishes are so well known – people have been making them for years and years, and they never go out of fashion! For the most part, I make these classics in the traditional way (why change a recipe that works?), but in some cases, I've given them a little twist. The **Chocolate orange bread & butter pudding,** for example, is definitely a twist on the original, but it's so deliciously rich and chocolatey that no-one can resist. I'd say the one closest to my heart is the **Lancashire hotpot**. I grew up in the North West of England (just a few miles outside of Lancashire), so I can confidently say I've had more than my fair share of this fantastic lamb dish!

Toad-in-the-hole with red onion gravy

Juicy pork sausages, baked in a glorious giant crispy Yorkshire pudding. I love the 'oohs' and 'ahhs' when I put this dinner on the table! And of course, what would sausages be without tasty gravy? So, I'm including my recipe for easy and flavourful red onion gravy too!

toad-in-the-hole

- 140g (1 cup + 1 tablespoon) plain (all-purpose) flour
- 4 medium eggs
- 200ml (¾ cup + 1 tablespoon) semi-skimmed (half-fat) milk
- 8 good-quality thick pork sausages
- 2 tablespoons sunflower oil
- ¼ teaspoon salt
- ¼ teaspoon ground black pepper

red onion gravy

- 1 tablespoon sunflower oil
- 1 tablespoon unsalted butter
- 2 large red onions, peeled and thinly sliced
- 2 teaspoons light brown sugar
- 2 tablespoons plain (all-purpose) flour
- 480ml (2 cups) hot beef stock (try to use a good-quality stock for the best flavour)
- 1 teaspoon Worcestershire sauce
- ¼ teaspoon salt
- ¼ teaspoon ground black pepper
- 10 sprigs of thyme (optional)

1. Make the Yorkshire pudding batter first. Place the flour in a large bowl and make a well in the centre.

2. Add the eggs and stir together with a balloon whisk, bringing the flour into the centre with the eggs bit-by-bit.

3. Add the milk and stir with a whisk until combined. It's fine if it's a little bit lumpy.

4. Place the bowl in the fridge for an hour (up to overnight) to chill. This is important to allow the flour granules to swell (also, cold batter hitting a very hot pan should result in a good rise).

5. Preheat the oven to 220°C/425°F/gas mark 9.

6. Place the sausages in a large baking dish. I find a metal or enamel dish is best for even heat distribution. You want one around 30 x 25 x 5cm (12 x 10 x 2in).

7. Drizzle the oil over the sausages, place in the oven and cook for 15–20 minutes, turning occasionally, until browned all over.

8. Take the Yorkshire pudding batter out of the fridge, season with salt and pepper and stir once more with a whisk.

9. Once the sausages are browned, open the oven door and carefully pour the batter into the baking dish, around the sausages. Close the door immediately and cook for 25–35 minutes, until risen and golden.

10. Meanwhile, make the gravy. Place the oil and butter in a frying pan (skillet) over a medium heat, until the butter has melted.

11. Add the onion and sugar to the pan and turn the heat down to medium-low. Cook the onions for about 15-20 minutes, stirring occasionally, until starting to caramelize.

12. Sprinkle over the flour and stir to coat the onion. Cook for 2 minutes to cook out the taste of the flour.

13. Add the hot beef stock slowly, whilst stirring all the time with a whisk, until the gravy thickens. Add a splash of Worcestershire sauce and season with salt and pepper.

14. Serve the toad-in-the-hole with the red onion gravy and sprinkle with sprigs of fresh thyme. I like to serve mine with greens, such as peas and cabbage, too.

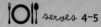
Traditional Lancashire hotpot

Lancashire Hotpot is a dish that remains hugely popular nearly 200 years after its creation. I grew up in the North of England, so this traditional Lancashire Hotpot, with tender chunks of lamb, all topped off with crisp slices of seasoned potatoes, is one of my staple dinners.

1 tablespoon unsalted butter

1 tablespoon sunflower oil

500g (1lb 2oz) lamb (not too lean - neck is best, but shoulder works well too), cut into bite-size chunks

2 onions, peeled and thinly sliced

1 heaped tablespoon plain (all-purpose) flour

480ml (2 cups) hot chicken or lamb stock (or 2 stock cubes with water)

2 bay leaves

½ teaspoon salt

½ teaspoon ground black pepper

1 tablespoon Worcestershire sauce

3 medium carrots, peeled and cut into chunks

680g (1½lb) floury potatoes, peeled and thinly sliced

1 tablespoon melted unsalted butter, for brushing

¼ teaspoon dried thyme

1. Preheat the oven to 170°C/325°F/gas mark 5.

2. Melt the butter and sunflower oil in an ovenproof frying pan (skillet) or shallow medium-size casserole pan and fry the lamb until lightly browned all over (about 3–4 minutes).

3. Using a slotted spoon, transfer the lamb to a bowl, then add the onion to the pan and cook for 3–4 minutes, stirring regularly, until soft.

4. Add the lamb back to the pan, stir in the flour and cook for a minute, while stirring.

5. Add the stock, bay leaves, salt, pepper and Worcestershire sauce. Give everything a stir and bring to the boil, then cover with a lid (or foil) and cook in the oven for 30 minutes.

6. After 30 minutes, remove the lid and stir in the carrots.

7. Layer the sliced potato on top, starting from the outside and moving toward the centre.

8. Brush the top of the potatoes with the melted butter and sprinkle over the dried thyme. Cover with a lid or foil and place back in the oven for 1 hour.

9. After an hour, turn the oven up to 200°C/400°F/gas mark 7 and remove the lid. Cook for a further 30 minutes until the potatoes are browned and crisp on top.

10. Take out of the oven and rest for 5 minutes or so (it will be very hot), then serve.

TIP You're looking for a cut of lamb with a little fat. Fat (not gristle) really helps to give this hotpot lots of lovely flavour. Diced lamb neck is perfect as it has little streaks of fat running through it. Diced lamb shoulder or leg will also work. If you want to use ready-diced lamb, that's fine too – just make sure it's a little fatty.

Classics

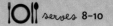
Shepherd's pie with rich gravy

My traditional shepherd's pie with creamy mash and rich gravy is just like my mum's! The perfect crispy top is just as important as that rich meat sauce. Serve with green vegetables, such as savoy cabbage, and pickled red cabbage.

- 1.8kg (4lb) floury potatoes, peeled and chopped into large chunks
- 2 tablespoons sunflower oil
- 2 onions, peeled and finely chopped
- 2 celery sticks, finely chopped
- 2 carrots, peeled and finely chopped
- 900g (2lb) minced (ground) lamb
- 1 teaspoon salt
- 1 teaspoon ground black pepper
- 2 tablespoons Worcestershire sauce
- 1 litre (4¼ cups) beef or lamb stock (or 3-4 stock cubes with water)
- 120ml (½ cup) double (heavy) cream
- 120g (8 tablespoons) unsalted butter
- 2 heaped tablespoons cornflour (cornstarch) mixed with 4 tablespoons cold water to make a slurry

1. Place the potato in a pan and cover with cold water. Bring to the boil and simmer for 15 minutes.

2. While the potato is cooking, preheat the oven to 200°C/400°F/gas mark 7.

3. Heat the oil in a large frying pan (skillet) over a medium heat.

4. Add the onion, celery and carrot and cook for 5 minutes, until they start to soften.

5. Add the minced lamb and cook until browned – breaking up any pieces as you go.

6. Add in half the salt and pepper, the Worcestershire sauce and stock and simmer for 5 minutes.

7. Drain the cooked potato and mash using a masher or ricer.

8. Add the cream, butter and remaining salt and pepper and mix together.

9. Slowly pour the cornflour slurry into the simmering lamb mixture, whilst stirring, to thicken the sauce.

10. Turn off the heat and use a slotted spoon to scoop out the lamb mixture and transfer to an ovenproof baking dish (30 x 20 x 3cm/13 x 9 x 2in). This should leave most of the gravy behind in the pan.

11. Top the lamb with the mashed potato, spreading it out and roughing up the top with a fork (so you get nice crispy bits).

12. Place the pie in the oven for 20 minutes, until the mashed potato is golden brown.

13. Heat up the gravy, then serve with the pie and some green veg and pickled red cabbage.

TIP Want to scale it down? I like to make a big batch and then freeze half of it, but you can halve the recipe to serve 4–5, or even quarter the recipe to serve 2. Stick to the same ratios but use a smaller baking dish for fewer people. However, the shepherd's pie should take the same amount of time to brown in the oven.

MAKE AHEAD Make the pie right up to the point before you put it in the oven. Then quickly cool, cover and refrigerate, along with the gravy, for up to 2 days. Place in the oven straight from the fridge, for 25–30 minutes at 200°C/400°F/gas mark 7 until the potato is golden brown and the meat sauce is starting to bubble up at the sides. Heat the gravy in a pan until piping hot.

Classics

Chicken stew & dumplings

Not your regular suet dumplings, these are super- easy, muffin-style dumplings that are a little lighter, and full of flavour. They top the tasty chicken and veggie-packed stew, making a whole meal, without the need for any sides.

8 skinless chicken thigh fillets (about 720g/1½lb), quartered

3 carrots, peeled and chopped into chunks

3 medium potatoes, peeled and chopped into small chunks

2 celery sticks, sliced

½ teaspoon salt

½ teaspoon ground black pepper

1 teaspoon dried thyme

1.2 litres (5 cups) chicken stock (or 3 stock cubes with water)

3 tablespoons unsalted butter

1 large onion, peeled and diced

50g (½ cup minus 1 tablespoon) plain (all-purpose) flour

dumplings

240g (1 cup) plain (all-purpose) flour

3 teaspoons baking powder

100g (1 cup) grated mature (sharp) Cheddar

½ teaspoon dried parsley

2 tablespoons unsalted butter,

180ml (¾ cup) milk

to serve

chopped flat-leaf parsley

1. Place the chicken, carrot, potato, celery, salt, pepper, thyme and stock in a large saucepan. Bring to the boil and allow to simmer for 15 minutes, then turn off the heat.

2. Preheat the oven to 190°C/ 375°F/gas mark 6.

3. When the chicken and vegetables are cooked, melt the butter in a large, deep casserole dish, over a medium heat. Add the onion and cook for 5–6 minutes, stirring often, until softened.

4. Add the flour and, using a balloon whisk, mix it into the onion and butter – it should form a creamy paste (a roux).

5. Allow the roux to cook for a minute whilst stirring with your whisk, then add in a ladle of the stock from the chicken broth (try to get mostly stock – not the chicken/veggies). Stir the broth into the mixture, using your whisk.

6. Repeat this until you have ladled out most of the stock from the chicken pan.

7. Bring the sauce to the boil and simmer gently, stirring for a couple of minutes, until the sauce thickens.

8. Pour the remaining stock, plus the chicken and vegetables, into the pan with the thickened sauce and allow to simmer for a few minutes, while you make the dumplings.

9. Place the flour, baking powder, cheese and parsley in a bowl and mix together.

10. Add the melted butter and three-quarters of the milk and stir together until you get a sticky dough – adding more milk if needed.

11. Take the chicken pan off the heat and, using two spoons, dollop large blobs of the dumpling mixture onto the top of the casserole.

12. Place in the oven and cook for 15–20 minutes, until the dumplings are lightly browned.

13. Take out of the oven and rest for 5 minutes before serving.

TIP Change up the dumplings by swapping out the Cheddar for your favourite cheese. Red Leicester or Parmesan work great. You can also add in ½ teaspoon garlic powder for garlic bread-style dumplings.

Slow-cooked Scottish beef stew

I love this rich and hearty beef stew. I first made it on Burns Night several years ago, and it's become a bit of a tradition ever since. Packed with melt-in-the-mouth chunks of beef and lots of veggies, it's filling and ultra-comforting on a cold evening.

2 tablespoons sunflower oil

1kg (2¼lb) braising beef (beef chuck), chopped into bite-size chunks

2 tablespoons plain (all-purpose) flour, mixed with a good pinch of salt and pepper

2 large onions, peeled and chopped

3 garlic cloves, peeled and minced

2 tablespoons red currant jelly or cranberry sauce

500ml (2 cups) red wine

2 large carrots, peeled and chopped

2 medium potatoes, peeled and chopped

½ small swede (rutagaba), peeled and chopped

720ml (3 cups) beef stock

2 tablespoons tomato purée (paste)

1 tablespoon Worcestershire sauce

4 bay leaves

2 teaspoons dark brown sugar

¾ teaspoon salt

¾ teaspoon ground black pepper

to serve
thyme sprigs
chunks of fresh bread

1. Preheat the oven to 165°C/325°F/gas mark 4.

2. Heat the oil in a large pan. Dust the chunks of beef in the flour and then fry for 7–8 minutes, until golden brown all over.

3. Add the onion and cook for a further 5 minutes.

4. Stir in the garlic, then add the red currant jelly and pour in the red wine. Simmer for 5 minutes.

5. Add the carrot, potato, swede, stock, tomato purée, Worcestershire sauce, bay leaves, sugar, salt and pepper.

6. Bring to a gentle boil, then cover with a lid and cook in the oven for 3–4 hours – stirring a couple of times during cooking. (Alternatively, you could transfer to a slow cooker and cook on high for 5–6 hours, or low for 7–8 hours.)

7. Serve topped with a little fresh thyme and some freshly cut bread.

TIP The best type of beef for this stew is braising steak – which comes from the forequarter. It consists of parts of the neck, shoulder blade and upper arm. It's a tough but very flavourful cut of meat. It has a lot of connective tissue, which needs long slow cooking to break down and become tender.

MAKE AHEAD You can make this stew, then cool, cover and refrigerate for up to 2 days. Reheat in a pan, on the hob (stovetop), until piping hot throughout.

Classics

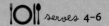
Rich slow-cooked steak pie

*You can't beat this rich, meaty and delicious homemade steak pie,
filled with slow-cooked beef and potatoes; it's the ultimate comfort food.*

1 tablespoon sunflower oil

1 large onion, peeled and chopped

500g (1lb 2oz) braising beef (beef
  chuck), chopped into bite-size
  chunks

1 tablespoon plain (all-purpose)
  flour

¾ teaspoon salt

¾ teaspoon ground black pepper

600ml (2½ cups) hot beef stock

2 large potatoes, peeled and
  and chopped (about
  300g/10½oz each)

1 teaspoon Worcestershire sauce

2 x 320g (2 x 11oz) packs of ready-
  rolled shortcrust pastry
  (pie dough)

1 egg, lightly whisked

1. Preheat the oven to 150°C/
300°F/gas mark 3.

2. Heat the oil in an ovenproof
casserole dish over a medium-low
heat and cook the onion for
5 minutes.

3. Place the beef in a bowl and mix
with the flour, plus ¼ teaspoon
each of the salt and pepper.

4. Add the beef to the pan with
the onion and cook over a medium
heat for about 5 minutes – until
the meat is sealed and slightly
browned all over. Give it a stir every
so often so the meat doesn't stick.

5. Add the beef stock and half the
potatoes.

6. Add the Worcestershire sauce
and remaining salt and pepper.
Bring to the boil, cover with a lid
and place in the oven for 1 hour.

7. After an hour, take out of the
oven, give it a stir and add the rest
of the potatoes. Add a splash of
hot stock or boiling water if the
meat is starting to look a little dry,
then return the dish to the oven
and cook for another hour.

8. Take out of the oven and turn
the oven up to 200°C/400°F/gas
mark 7. Stir the casserole again,
then set aside to cool slightly for
5 minutes before assembling
the pie.

9. Take a 25cm (10in) round pie
dish and line it with one sheet of
pastry, so it overhangs the edge of
the dish slightly.

10. Spoon the pie mixture into
the dish and top the pie with the
remaining pastry sheet.

11. Crimp the edges of the pastry
by pinching it all the way round
between your finger and thumb.

12. Cut off any excess pastry and
brush the top all over with egg
wash. If you have any holes in the
top of the pie, make a few leaves
out of the excess pastry to cover
them up. Egg-wash the leaves too.

13. Use a knife to pierce a couple
of holes in the centre of the pie –
to allow any steam to escape.

14. Place the pie in the oven
for 30–35 minutes, until golden
brown.

15. Serve with your favourite
vegetables.

TIP Want extra gravy? Add
500ml (2 cups) extra stock
when cooking the filling. Use
a slotted spoon to transfer the
filling to the pastry-lined dish
and the sauce that's left in the
pan will be your gravy. Cover
and reheat it just before serving.

Classics

129

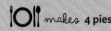
Cheese & onion pies

Growing up, I used to love a cheese and onion pie from the chip shop. The way the cheesy filling oozed out – delicious! They don't seem to sell them in many chippies anymore, so I've created my own, and it's just as oozy and even more cheesy and delicious than the original!

- 2 x 320g (2 x 11oz) packs of ready-rolled shortcrust pastry (pie dough)
- 1 medium potato (about 200g/7oz), peeled and cut into 1cm (½in) cubes
- 2 tablespoons unsalted butter
- 1 large onion, peeled and finely sliced
- 2 tablespoons plain (all-purpose) flour
- 180ml (¾ cup) milk
- 50ml (2 tablespoons +1 teaspoon) double (heavy) cream
- 150g (1½ cups) mature (sharp) Cheddar, grated
- ¼ teaspoon mustard powder
- ¼ teaspoon salt
- ½ teaspoon ground black pepper
- 1 egg lightly whisked

1. Preheat the oven to 200°C/400°F/gas mark 7.
2. Unroll one of the pastry sheets and slice into four squares (we'll use the leftover to fill any gaps).
3. Line four individual 10cm (4in) round pie dishes with the pastry, so that it covers the base and sides and overhangs slightly. Cover any gaps with the leftover pastry.
4. Use a fork to prick several holes in the base.
5. Cover each pie case with baking parchment and fill with baking beans (or use dried beans or rice).
6. Place the pies on a tray (sheet) and bake in the oven for 10 minutes to par-cook the pastry.
7. Remove the pie bases from the oven, leave to cool for 10 minutes, then carefully remove the parchment and baking beans.
8. While the bases are cooking, then cooling, make the filling.
9. Place the potato in a saucepan and cover with water. Bring to the boil and simmer for 10–12 minutes – until the potato is very tender and starting to break apart. Drain and set aside.
10. Melt the butter in a second saucepan and cook the onion, stirring, over a medium heat for 5 minutes, until it softens.
11. Sprinkle over the flour, stir to coat and cook for a further minute.
12. Add the milk a splash at a time, whilst stirring, until the milk is fully incorporated.
13. Add the cream, cheese, mustard powder, salt and pepper, along with the cooked potato.
14. Stir together until the cheese has melted and the potato breaks down. The filling should be thick and only just pourable; stir in a splash of milk if it looks too thick.
15. Divide the filling among the four pie cases.
16. Using a pair of scissors, tidy up the the edges of the cooked pastry, then brush the rim with a little of the egg wash.
17. Unroll the second sheet of pastry. Slice into four squares and place one on top of each pie dish.
18. Cut off any overhang with scissors, then crimp the edges together, using a fork.
19. Brush the tops of the pies with egg wash and pierce two holes in the middle, using a sharp knife.
20. Place the pies on a baking tray and bake in the oven for 20-25 minutes, until golden brown.

Classics

131

Creamy fish pie

A luxuriously rich dinner with plenty of fish and juicy prawns
in a creamy sauce, all topped off with cheesy mashed potato.
It freezes well, so I like to make up a double batch, then serve one and freeze one.

1kg (2lb 3oz) floury potatoes, peeled and chopped into large chunks
3 tablespoons unsalted butter
3 tablespoons double (heavy) cream
a large pinch of salt and pepper
600ml (2½ cups) milk
2 salmon fillets
2 cod or haddock fillets
12-18 king (jumbo) prawns (shrimp) these can be cooked or raw (make sure they're de-veined)
2 tablespoons plain (all-purpose) flour
150g (1½ cups) grated mature (sharp) Cheddar

to serve
1 tablespoon chopped chives

1. Preheat the oven to 200°C/400°F/gas mark 7.
2. Place the potato in a pan and cover with cold water. Bring to the boil and simmer for 15 minutes.
3. Drain the potato, then mash with a potato masher or ricer. Stir in half of the butter, the cream and salt and pepper, then set aside.
4. Place the milk in a large saucepan with the salmon and cod/haddock. Bring to the boil and simmer for 3 minutes. If you're using raw prawns, add them in for the last minute of cooking. After 3 minutes, your fish should be cooked and starting to flake apart.
5. Using a slotted spoon, transfer the flaked fish and prawns (add the cold, cooked prawns at this point, if using) to a large baking dish. Remove and discard the skin if the fish wasn't skinless.
6. Pour the cooking liquid into a jug and set aside
7. To make the sauce, melt the remaining butter in a saucepan, then stir in the flour. Heat through over a medium heat for a minute, whilst stirring with a whisk or wooden spoon.
8. Slowly add the reserved cooking liquid, still stirring with a whisk (don't whisk it hard though, or you'll end up with a frothy sauce).

The sauce will begin to thicken after a few minutes.
9. Turn off the heat and stir through half the cheese and a pinch of black pepper.
10. Now it's time to assemble the pie. Pour the sauce over the fish/prawn mixture in the dish.
11. Spoon the mashed potato over the top and use a fork to spread it out and rough up the top (for a crispy finish).
12. Sprinkle over the remaining cheese and place in the oven for 15–20 minutes, until the cheese is melted and golden.
13. Top with chopped chives and serve. I like mine with peas and sweetcorn.

MAKE AHEAD Make the dish up, but don't place in the oven. Cool, cover and refrigerate or freeze. If freezing, defrost thoroughly overnight in the refrigerator. To reheat, place in the oven at 200°C/400°F/gas mark 7 for 30-35 minutes (the dish will need this if reheating straight from the refrigerator), until piping hot throughout. Cover the dish for the first half of the cooking time, then remove to allow the mashed potato to brown.

Classics

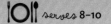

Big-batch sausage & bean one-pot

A sausage casserole with a warming, spicy kick – using regular pork sausage AND chorizo. I love serving this at the table with a big bowl of mashed potato.

2 tablespoons sunflower oil

20 good-quality chipolata
 sausages (or thin pork sausages)

1 large red onion, peeled and
 roughly chopped

2 red (bell) peppers, deseeded
 and roughly chopped

20 mini chorizo (the bite-size
 ones), cut in half

3 garlic cloves, peeled and minced

2 teaspoons paprika

1 teaspoon dried thyme

120m (½ cup) red wine

2 chicken stock cubes, crumbled

3 x 400g (3x 14oz) cans chopped
 tomatoes

1 x 400g (14oz) can haricot (navy)
 beans, drained and rinsed

1 x 400g (14oz) can cannellini
 beans, drained and rinsed

to serve
mashed potato

1. Heat the oil in a large, non-stick frying pan (skillet) until hot, then brown the sausages all over (you may need to do this in two batches). It should take about 6–8 minutes.

2. Add the onion and cook for a further 3 minutes over a medium heat, until the onion softens slightly.

3. Add the pepper and mini chorizo pieces and cook for a further 3 minutes (make sure the chorizo has contact with the pan, rather than resting on top of everything else; this will help it to brown slightly).

4. Add the garlic, paprika and thyme and stir. Cook for 1 minute, then add the wine. Let the wine bubble for 2–3 minutes until reduced, scraping any bits that have stuck to the bottom of the pan as these add extra flavour.

5. Crumble in the stock cubes and stir, then add in the canned tomato. Stir and bring to a gentle boil. Turn down the heat and simmer for 15 minutes, stirring a couple of times during cooking.

6. Add in the drained haricot and cannellini beans, stir, and cook for a further 5 minutes, until heated through.

7. Serve with mashed potato.

TIP Make it in the slow cooker. Crumble in the stock cubes and add the canned tomato at step 5. Bring to the boil, then transfer to your slow cooker and cook for 6 hours on low, or 3 hours on high. Finally, stir in the beans and cook for a further 30 minutes on high.

MAKE AHEAD Cook the whole dish, then cool, cover and refrigerate for up to 2 days. Take out of the fridge an hour or two before you want to reheat, just to take the chill off the dish. Reheat on the hob (stovetop) over a medium heat for about 20 minutes. Keep the dish covered for the first 10 minutes, then remove the lid and stir every couple of minutes to fully disperse the heat. Ensure the sausages are piping hot throughout before serving.

Classics

Bubble & squeak

Bubble and squeak is such a great way to use up roast dinner leftovers. If you've got roast potatoes or other vegetables, such as peas, carrots or sprouts, throw them in too!

200g (3 cups) leftover chopped cooked cabbage (this doesn't have to be exact); I like to use savoy cabbage

700g (3 cups) leftover mashed potato (again, this doesn't have to be exact)

¼ teaspoon salt

¼ teaspoon ground black pepper

2 tablespoons butter, salted or unsalted

2 tablespoons sunflower oil

serving suggestions

chopped flat-leaf parsley

6 rashers (strips) grilled crispy bacon, chopped

poached or fried eggs

brown sauce

1. Preheat the grill (broiler).
2. In a bowl, mix the cabbage with the mashed potato, salt and pepper.
3. Add a tablespoon of butter and a tablespoon of oil to a large 30cm (12in) frying pan (skillet). Or use two medium-size pans, if you prefer.
4. Heat the pan over a medium-high heat until the butter has melted and is bubbling.
5. Add the bubble and squeak mixture to the pan and, using a spatular squash it down to completely cover the base of the pan. Using a fork, ruffle the top of the bubble and squeak (the more ruffles, the more crispy bits).
6. Fry for 5–7 minutes, until the edges start to brown.
7. Melt the remaining 1 tablespoon butter and mix with the remaining 1 tablespoon oil, then brush the top of the bubble and squeak with the mixture.
8. Place under the grill and grill (broil) for 4–5 minutes, until golden brown.
9. Remove from the grill and sprinkle with a little salt and pepper and some chopped parsley.
10. Serve as-is, or sprinkle with chopped crispy bacon and top with poached/fried eggs.
11. Serve the bubble and squeak with brown sauce, if you like.

TIP Make it vegetarian by serving without the bacon, or by replacing the bacon with vegetarian bacon.

Classics

136

Cornish pasties

The Cornish pasty comprises tender, peppery beef mixed with melt-in-your-mouth vegetables, all wrapped up in buttery golden pastry. I completely understand why Cornish folk have so much pride in this hand-held meal.

pastry

- 450g (3⅔ cups) plain (all-purpose) flour, plus extra for rolling out and sprinkling
- 2 teaspoons baking powder
- 1 teaspoon salt
- 125g (½ cup + 1 teaspoon) unsalted butter, chopped into chunks
- 2 egg yolks
- 125ml (½ cup +1 teaspoon) cold water

filling

- 450g (1lb) potatoes, peeled and finely diced
- 150g (5½oz) swede (rutagaba), peeled and finely diced
- 150g (5½oz) onion, peeled and finely chopped
- 300g (11oz) skirt steak, finely chopped, with fat discarded (weigh the meat after discarding the fat)
- 1 teaspoon salt
- 1 teaspoon ground black pepper
- 45g (3 tablespoons) unsalted butter, chopped into small cubes
- 1 egg, beaten

1. To make your pastry, place the flour, baking powder and salt in a food processor and give it a quick mix.

2. Add the butter and whizz until the mixture resembles breadcrumbs.

3. Add the egg yolks and mix. Then, with the motor on, add the water a bit at a time until the dough comes together into a ball. You may not need all the water.

4. Take the dough out of the food processor, wrap in clingfilm (plastic wrap) or wax paper and refrigerate for an hour.

5. Preheat the oven to 180°C/350°F/gas mark 6. Sprinkle flour on two large baking trays (sheets).

6. Roll out your chilled pastry onto a floured surface, until about 3mm (⅛in) thick.

7. Using a round 20cm (8in) plate as a template, cut out circles. Re-roll and repeat until you run out of dough. Stack the circles onto a plate, using a sprinkling of flour between each layer.

8. In a large bowl, mix the potato, swede, onion and steak together with salt and pepper.

9. Place one of your dough circles onto a work surface and arrange a good handful of the meat mixture onto half of the circle, leaving a 2cm (¾in) border around the

edge. It'll look like a lot of mixture, but it needs to be packed full.

10. Dot 1½ teaspoons butter on top of the meat and veg pile.

11. Using a pastry brush, paint a little egg wash around the edge of the circle. This will help the pastry to stick together.

12. Now fold the other side of the pastry over the meat until the edges meet and you have a semi-circle. Seal firmly and crimp with your fingers.

13. Transfer the pasty (turnover) to the baking tray and, with a sharp knife, make a little hole in the top to let out the steam. Repeat with the remaining pasties.

14. Brush the remaining egg wash over the top of the pasties and place in the oven for 50 minutes, until golden brown.

15. Take out of the oven and leave to cool for 5 minutes before eating.

TIP You can replace the pastry with shop-bought shortcrust pastry (pie dough).

MAKE AHEAD Refrigerate the cooked pasties. Preheat the oven to 190°C/375°F/gas mark 6 and cook for 30 minutes, until piping hot throughout.

Classics

139

Sticky toffee pudding

*Fluffy treacle and date sponge, topped with a lusciously rich toffee sauce –
this is one of my absolute favourite desserts of all time. There's no way you're leaving
the table without two servings of this ultimate British dessert.*

150g (approx. ⅔ cup) Medjool
   dates, pitted and finely chopped
150ml (⅔ cup) boiling water
90g (6 tablespoons) unsalted
   butter, softened
120g (⅔ cup) light brown sugar
2 eggs
2 teaspoons vanilla extract
2 tablespoons black treacle
   (blackstrap molasses)
190g (1½ cups + 1 tablespoon)
   plain (all-purpose) flour
1½ teaspoons baking powder
½ teaspoon bicarbonate of soda
   (baking soda)
a pinch of salt
120ml (½ cup) milk

toffee sauce

175g (¾ cup + 2 tablespoons)
   light muscovado sugar
60g (4 tablespoons) unsalted
   butter, chopped into pieces
240ml (1 cup) double (heavy)
   cream
1 tablespoon black treacle

to serve
vanilla ice cream

1. Lightly grease your baking dish.
I use a 28 x 18 x 4cm (11 x 7 x 1½in)
dish but a square 23cm (9in) dish
will also work.

2. Place the dates and water in
a bowl and leave to soak for
10 minutes. After 10 minutes,
use a fork to squish the dates
(don't drain).

3. Preheat the oven to 170°C/
325°F/gas mark 5.

4. In a large bowl, beat together
the butter and sugar until creamy,
then mix in the eggs, one at a
time. Stir in the vanilla extract
and treacle.

5. Add half the flour, the baking
powder, bicarbonate of soda, salt
and half the milk. Stir gently to
combine, then add the remaining
flour and milk. Stir again until just
combined.

6. Add the mashed-up date
mixture (including the liquid).
Stir, then spoon into the prepared
baking dish.

7. Cook in the oven for 25–35
minutes, until firm on top.

8. About 10 minutes before the
cake is ready, make the toffee
sauce. Place the sugar and butter
in a medium saucepan with half
the cream.

9. Bring to the boil over a medium
heat, stirring all the time, until the
sugar has completely dissolved.

10. Stir in the black treacle, turn
up the heat slightly and let the
mixture bubble for 2–3 minutes,
until it turns a light-brown toffee
colour. Stir occasionally to ensure
it doesn't burn.

11. Take the pan off the heat and
stir in the rest of the cream, then
set aside.

12. Take the sponge out of the
oven and pour half of the toffee
sauce over the sponge.

13. Serve with the remaining
toffee sauce and some vanilla ice
cream.

TIP Add ½ teaspoon sea salt to
the toffee sauce for a salted sticky
toffee pudding.

MAKE AHEAD You can make
the whole dessert ahead, then
cool, cover and refrigerate for
up to 2 days. You can store the
remaining sauce, covered, in the
fridge too. Reheat in portions,
uncovered, in the microwave, until
piping hot. It should take about
30–45 seconds per piece. Reheat
the remaining sauce in a pan,
until piping hot.

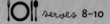
Chocolate orange bread & butter pudding

Rich, chocolatey and zesty, this bread and butter pudding is a twist on the classic, with a sweet, crisp exterior and a beautiful soft-and-tender centre.

300g (10½oz) white bloomer-style bread

3 tablespoons unsalted butter

100g (¾ cup) candied peel chunks

100g (⅔ cup) sultanas (golden raisins)

240ml (1 cup) milk

300ml (1¼ cups) double (heavy) cream

1 teaspoon vanilla extract

4 egg yolks

100g (½ cup) light brown sugar

2 tablespoons cornflour (cornstarch)

1 teaspoon Valencian orange extract

150g (5½oz) dark chocolate, chopped

80g (½ cup) chocolate chips

1 orange, sliced

1. Grease a large ovenproof casserole dish (I use an oval 28 x 25cm/11 x 10in dish).

2. Slice the bread into 2½cm (1in) thick slices and spread with the butter, then cut each slice into 2½cm (1in) chunks.

3. Arrange the bread chunks in the casserole dish and sprinkle over the candied peel and sultanas, then set aside.

4. In a saucepan, heat the milk, cream and vanilla extract, until almost boiling, then turn off the heat.

5. Meanwhile, place the egg yolks, brown sugar and cornflour in a large jug and mix together.

6. Stirring with a whisk, add a splash of the milk mixture to the egg-sugar mixture. Continue to add, a splash at a time, and keep stirring with the whisk, until the milk has all been added.

7. Give the milk pan a wash to remove any residues, then pour the milk and egg mixture back into the pan. Whilst slowly stirring with a whisk, heat over a medium heat until the mixture thickens.

8. Turn off the heat and stir in the orange extract and dark chocolate, until it melts.

9. Spoon the chocolate mixture over the bread in the casserole dish and mix it together to coat the bread.

10. Leave to sit for 30 minutes. Meanwhile, preheat the oven to 175°C/350°F/gas mark 6.

11. Sprinkle the chocolate chips over the bread mixture, then place the dish in the oven for 25–30 minutes, until the edges of the bread are crisp.

12. Remove from the oven and arrange the orange slices over the top. Serve on its own or with ice cream.

TIP Swap out the peel and/or the sultanas for different types of dried fruit. Cranberries, raisins and dried blueberries all work really well.

Classics

Slow cooked.

Time is your friend with these recipes; allowing the flavours to develop and guaranteeing a tasty finish. Some of them are made in the slow cooker, while others are cooked slowly in the oven or on the hob. A bit of prep beforehand, and you can let everything cook leisurely while you get on with other things. For a casserole with a difference, try my **Steak Diane casserole** with brandy and cream. It's so good, I've even served it at dinner parties. The **Beef ragù** makes a really special dinner, served up with pappardelle pasta. The slow-cooker **Short ribs** are a great way to make an inexpensive cut of meat taste amazing. I always make enough for leftovers, then shred up the meat and use it to make burritos.

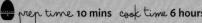
Slow-cooker lentil soup with crispy tortillas

This nutritious soup is packed with vegetables and creamy red lentils.
I love to top it off with some crispy tortilla strips to add a bit of crunch too.

1 onion, peeled and finely diced

1 red (bell) pepper, deseeded and finely diced

3 carrots, peeled and chopped into small pieces

2 medium Maris Piper potatoes, peeled and chopped into small cubes

100g (½ cup) red lentils

720ml (3 cups) vegetable stock

½ teaspoon salt

¼ teaspoon ground black pepper

60g (2 packed cups) baby spinach

75g (¾ cup) grated Cheddar

crispy tortillas

1 tablespoon olive oil

½ teaspoon garlic salt

½ teaspoon dried parsley

1 plain tortilla wrap

1. Place the onion, pepper, carrot, potato, red lentils, stock, salt and pepper in the slow cooker.

2. Cook on high for 4 hours, or low for 6 hours.

3. While the soup is cooking, make the crispy tortillas. Preheat the oven to 200°C/400°F/gas mark 7.

4. In a small bowl, mix together the olive oil, garlic salt and dried parsley and brush onto one side of the tortilla.

5. Slice the tortilla into thin strips or wedges, then place on a baking tray (sheet) in a single layer.

6. Bake in the oven for 5–7 minutes, until crisp, then remove and allow to cool.

7. When the soup is ready, stir in the baby spinach and Cheddar.

8. Divide among bowls and top with pieces of crispy tortilla.

TIP Add a pinch of chilli (red pepper) flakes and smoked paprika to the tortilla strips for a smoky spicy flavour.

MAKE AHEAD You can make this soup ahead, then cool, cover and refrigerate for 2-3 days. Reheat in a pan on the hob (stovetop), until piping hot.

Slow-cooked

Slow-cooker chicken & vegetable soup

This simple, hearty comfort food is a great way to make a tasty, nutritious meal out of inexpensive cuts of meat. I love to serve it with a big wedge of fresh bread.

4 bone-in, skin-on chicken thighs

4 chicken drumsticks

1 onion, peeled and finely chopped

2 garlic cloves, peeled and minced

2 celery sticks, sliced

3 medium carrots, roughly chopped

2 medium potatoes, peeled and chopped into bite-size chunks

1 bay leaf

¼ teaspoon salt

½ teaspoon ground black pepper

1 litre (4¼ cups) strong chicken stock (I used water plus 4 stock cubes)

to serve

chopped flat-leaf parsley or thyme

crusty bread

1. Place the chicken thighs, chicken drumsticks, onion, garlic, celery, carrot, potato, bay leaf, salt, pepper and chicken stock in the slow cooker.

2. Place the lid on and cook for 6 hours on low, or 4 hours on high.

3. Remove the lid and, using a set of tongs, transfer the chicken thighs and drumsticks to a chopping (cutting) board. Remove and discard the bay leaf.

4. Remove the chicken skin and then, using two forks, shred the meat.

5. Place the chicken meat back into the slow cooker and stir together.

6. Divide the chicken soup among bowls and top with fresh parsley or thyme.

7. Serve with a big wedge of crusty bread.

MAKE AHEAD You can make the soup, then cool, cover and refrigerate. Reheat in a pan until piping hot.

Slow-cooked

149

Slow-cooker chicken casserole

A warming, delicious, slow-cooked chicken casserole with fall-apart meat, lovely veggies and a seasoned creamy sauce. Most of the work is done in the slow cooker, so you can look forward to a hearty family dinner at the end of the day.

2 tablespoons sunflower oil

8 boneless chicken thigh fillets (about 720g/1½lb), trimmed of fat

2 tablespoons unsalted butter

2 small onions, peeled and diced

3 garlic cloves, peeled and minced

3 tablespoons plain (all-purpose) flour

1 teaspoon salt

1 teaspoon ground black pepper

1 teaspoon dried thyme

½ teaspoon celery salt

480ml (2 cups) chicken stock

1 tablespoon lemon juice (juice of ½ lemon)

20 baby chestnut (cremini) mushrooms

20 Chantenay carrots, scrubbed

3 celery sticks, roughly chopped

60ml (¼ cup) double (heavy) cream

a small bunch of flat-leaf parsley, chopped

1. Heat the oil in a large frying pan (skillet) over a medium-high heat.

2. Add the chicken thighs and lightly brown on both sides – this should take about 5 minutes – then transfer to a slow cooker.

3. Melt the butter in the pan and cook the onion for 5 minutes, stirring occasionally, until softened.

4. Add the garlic, stir and cook for a further minute.

5. Stir in the flour, salt, pepper, thyme and celery salt and cook for 2 minutes.

6. Add the stock and lemon juice, whilst stirring. Bring to the boil, then pour into the slow cooker over the top of the chicken.

7. Add the mushrooms, carrots and celery to the slow cooker and stir.

8. Place the lid on and cook on a low heat for 5–6 hours, or a high heat for 3–4 hours.

9. Once cooked, use two forks to shred the chicken a little, then stir in the cream.

10. Serve topped with fresh parsley.

TIP Want to cook it in the oven? Cook in a casserole dish, covered with a lid, at 175°C/350°F/ gas mark 6 for 45–60 minutes, until the carrots are tender. Add 120ml (½ cup) extra chicken stock when making the sauce, as liquid evaporates more in the oven. Also, check and stir the dish a couple of times when cooking in the oven.

MAKE AHEAD You can make this dish ahead, then cool, cover and refrigerate. Heat through in a large saucepan for 10–15 minutes over a medium heat until the chicken is hot all the way through. Add a splash of cream or milk to loosen it up, if needed.

Slow-cooked

Big-batch creamy chicken & mushroom one-pan casserole

This is a big-batch meal, so you can eat some and freeze some for a quick meal on another day. If you don't want to make a batch this big, you can halve the ingredients with no change to the cooking times. Cook this dish on the hob (stovetop) or in the oven.

5 chicken breasts (1kg/2¼lb), chopped into bite-size pieces
70g (²⁄₃ cup) plain (all-purpose) flour
1 teaspoon salt
1 teaspoon ground black pepper
2 tablespoons sunflower oil
2 tablespoons unsalted butter
3 onions, peeled and finely diced
5 garlic cloves, peeled and minced
1 teaspoon dried thyme
½ teaspoon celery salt (optional)
1 litre (4¼ cups) chicken stock
300ml (1¼ cups) milk
2 tablespoons lemon juice (juice from 1 lemon)
20 chestnut (cremini) mushrooms, thickly sliced (white mushrooms or baby portabello are good too)
240ml (1 cup) double (heavy) cream
a small bunch of flat-leaf parsley, chopped

1. Place the chicken in a bowl with 45g (6 tablespoons) of the flour plus ½ teaspoon each of salt and pepper. Toss to cover the chicken in the flour and seasoning.

2. Heat the oil in a large frying pan (skillet) over a high heat and, working in two or three batches, add the chicken. Brown all over (it doesn't need to be cooked through at this point). Using a slotted spoon, transfer to a bowl.

3. Melt the butter in the same frying pan over a medium heat. Add the onion, garlic, thyme and celery salt and cook for 5–10 minutes, until the onion softens. Sprinkle over the remaining flour and stir for a minute (it will be lumpy).

4. Pour in a splash of the stock and stir, using a whisk, until combined. Continue to add stock, a little at a time, whilst stirring, until all the stock is added and you have a smooth sauce with no lumps (besides the onion).

5. Add the milk and continue to stir over the heat until the sauce thickens.

6. Add the lemon juice, mushroom, chicken and the remaining salt and pepper.

7. Stir together, then cover with a lid and simmer gently on the hob (stovetop) for 20 minutes. Alternatively, you can transfer to a casserole dish at this point. Cover with foil and place in the oven at 175°C/350°F/gas mark 6 for 30 minutes.

8. Remove the lid and stir in the cream, then heat through for a further 5 minutes (or place back in the oven if oven cooking).

9. Serve the casserole with your favourite vegetables and a sprinkling of parsley.

MAKE AHEAD Make the dish, then cool, cover and refrigerate for up to a day. Heat through thoroughly in the oven, covered, at 175°C/350°F/gas mark 6 for 20–25 minutes. Or heat through on the hob (stovetop) for 10–15 minutes over a medium heat, until the chicken is hot all the way through. Add a splash of cream or milk to loosen it up, if needed.

Beef ragù

*Slow-cooked, fall-apart beef in a rich red wine and tomato sauce.
Just 10 minutes of prep needed, then leave it to cook in the oven or slow cooker.
I love to make a big batch, so I have leftovers for freezing.
It's such a versatile and flavourful recipe – perfect for cosying up in front of
the TV with a bowl, or serving as the main course at a dinner party.*

1kg (2¼lb) braising beef, (beef chuck), chopped
3 heaped tablespoons plain (all-purpose) flour
½ teaspoon salt
½ teaspoon ground black pepper
3 tablespoons sunflower oil
2 onions, peeled and chopped
4 medium carrots, peeled and chopped into small chunks
3 celery sticks, finely chopped
3 garlic cloves, peeled and minced
2 tablespoons tomato purée (paste)
300ml (1¼ cups) red wine
2 x 400g (2 x 14oz) cans chopped tomatoes
600ml (2½ cups) hot beef stock (or 2 stock cubes plus water)
1 teaspoon dried thyme

to serve
cooked pappardelle pasta
grated Parmesan
a small bunch of flat-lef parsley, chopped
chunks of crusty bread

1. Preheat the oven to 160°C/320°F/gas mark 4.
2. Place the braising beef in a bowl and mix with the flour, salt and pepper.
3. Heat the oil in a large casserole pan over a medium-high heat.
4. Brown the beef (you may need to do this in two or three batches). It should take about 4–5 minutes per batch.
5. Add all the beef back into the pan, add the onion and cook over a low heat for 3–4 minutes, until the onion starts to soften.
6. Add the carrot, celery and garlic and cook for another 2 minutes.
7. Add in the tomato purée and stir, then add in the wine, turn up the heat and let it bubble for a couple of minutes. Scrape any bits that may have stuck to the bottom of the pan – this adds so much flavour.
8. Add in the canned tomato, beef stock and thyme. Bring to the boil, stir and then cover the pan with a lid.
9. Place in the oven for 3–4 hours, until the beef is very tender. Check a couple of times during the final hour, to ensure the sauce isn't running dry. If so, top up with a splash of boiling water.

10. Once cooked, serve with pappardelle. You can stir the pasta through the sauce or just serve the sauce on top; whichever you prefer.
11. Top with a sprinkling of Parmesan and parsley, then serve with chunks of crusty bread.

TIP If you want to cook this in a slow cooker, reduce the amount of stock to 480ml (2 cups). This is because the liquid doesn't evaporate in the slow cooker as much as it does in the oven. Make the recipe, up to and including the point where you add the canned tomato, stock and thyme. Bring to the boil, then pour everything into the slow cooker and cook on low for 6-8 hours, or high for 4-5 hours.

MAKE AHEAD Make the ragù, then cool quickly, cover and refrigerate for up to 2 days. Reheat in a saucepan over a medium heat, stirring occasionally, until piping hot throughout.

Slow-cooked

Chilli con carne

This is actually my husband's recipe, and the whole family adores it. The perfect blend of spices, beans and extra veggies means you can make a pound of minced beef feed eight people! Best served with rice, coriander, sour cream, chopped red chillies and purple corn chips.

2 tablespoons sunflower oil

2 large onions, peeled and diced

6 garlic cloves, peeled and minced

500g (1lb 2oz) minced (ground) beef

360ml (1½ cups) red wine

180ml (¾ cup) beef stock

4 tablespoons Worcestershire sauce

2 tablespoons honey

2 red (bell) peppers, deseeded and chopped

4 x 400g (4 x 14oz) cans chopped tomatoes

1 teaspoon smoked paprika

4 teaspoons ground cumin

2 teaspoons ground coriander

2 teaspoons hot chilli powder

3 teaspoons ground ginger

2 teaspoons mixed herbs

½ teaspoon salt

½ teaspoon ground black pepper

1 chopped chilli

3 tablespoons tomato purée (paste)

1 tablespoon tomato ketchup

1 teaspoon chipotle paste

2 chunks of 80% dark chocolate

2 x 400g (14oz) cans kidney beans, drained and rinsed

1 x 420g (14oz) can mixed beans, drained and rinsed

a small bunch of fresh coriander (cilantro), chopped

1. Heat the oil in a large casserole pan over a medium-high heat.

2. Add the onion and cook for 5–6 minutes, until soft and translucent.

3. Add the garlic and cook for a further minute.

4. Add the beef and cook until just browned. Break any large pieces up with a wooden spoon.

5. Add the red wine, bring to a bubble and simmer for 3 minutes.

6. Add in the stock, Worcestershire sauce and honey and give it a stir.

7. Add in the peppers and cook for another minute, then stir in the canned tomato.

8. Add the smoked paprika, cumin, ground coriander, chilli powder, ginger, mixed herbs, salt and pepper and the chopped fresh chilli. Give it all a mix and cook for 2–3 minutes.

9. Add the tomato purée, tomato ketchup, chipotle paste and dark chocolate. Stir and bring to a simmer, then loosely cover and simmer for 1 hour.

10. After an hour, add in the kidney beans and mixed beans. Give them a stir and allow the chilli to simmer for another 20 minutes (this is also a good time to put your rice on if you're serving it with rice).

11. Finally, stir in the chopped coriander just before serving.

12. Serve with rice, extra coriander, sour cream and chopped fresh chillies, if you like.

13. I also like to serve mine with a few purple corn chips.

TIP Although we often serve it with rice, it's also great with pasta, on tortilla chips or jacket potatoes. I even sometimes use a portion from the freezer to make a quick, spicy lasagne.

MAKE AHEAD I think it tastes even better when made ahead and reheated, as it allows the flavours to develop even further. Once cooked, cool quickly, cover and refrigerate for up to 2 days, or freeze. Defrost overnight in the refrigerator. Reheat in a pan or the microwave until piping hot throughout.

Slow-cooked

Beef bourguignon

A sumptuously rich, slow-cooked beef stew, braised with red wine and topped with crispy pancetta; this makes such a stunning-yet-comforting winter dinner.

1 tablespoon sunflower oil

120g (½ cup) bacon lardons

20 small shallots, peeled, 6 of them cut in half, the rest left whole

1.4kg (3lb) beef braising steak, (beef chuck), cut into large chunks

3 tablespoons plain (all-purpose) flour

½ teaspoon salt

½ teaspoon ground black pepper

1 tablespoon tomato purée (paste)

1 x 750ml (25fl oz) bottle red wine (it doesn't have to be an expensive wine; I use Shiraz)

240ml (1 cup) beef stock

3 bay leaves

1 teaspoon dried thyme

16-20 Chantenay carrots, peeled or scrubbed

150g (2 cups) chestnut (cremini) mushrooms, thickly sliced

1. Preheat the oven to 160°C/320°F/gas mark 4.

2. Heat the oil in a large ovenproof casserole dish over a medium heat and add the lardons. Fry until golden brown, then transfer to a bowl using a slotted spoon.

3. Add the halved shallots to the pan and fry over a high heat for a few minutes, until seared, then transfer to the bowl with the lardons.

4. There should still be 2-3 tablespoons of oil left in the pan at this point. If there isn't, top up with a little more oil.

5. In a bowl, toss the beef with the flour, salt and pepper.

6. In three or four batches, brown the beef in the pan over a medium–high heat (about 5–6 minutes per batch). Transfer each cooked batch to a bowl, before starting on the next batch.

7. When cooked, return all the beef to the pan and stir in the tomato purée.

8. Add the wine, stock, bay leaves, thyme, carrot, mushroom and the whole shallots. Give everything a stir and scrape any bits that may have stuck to the bottom of the pan – this adds so much flavour.

9. Bring to the boil, then turn off the heat. Cover the pan with a lid and place in the oven to cook for 3 hours. Check a couple of times to make sure the bourguignon isn't going dry. If so, add half a cup of water.

10. After 3 hours, stir the bacon lardons and fried shallots into the pan, place the lid back on and return to the oven for another 10 minutes to heat through.

11. Serve with your favourite vegetables.

TIP Some people will say to use the best wine possible. Personally, I think go with something fairly inexpensive, as the flavour will mellow out during cooking anyway. Don't go with anything too vinegary though.

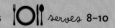
Steak Diane casserole

A great way to get the flavours of Steak Diane, but with tasty, fall-apart chunks of beef (much more cost-effective too!). It's a change from a regular beef casserole and the addition of brandy makes it extra special.

2 tablespoons sunflower oil

1½kg (3⅓lb) braising beef, chopped into bite-size chunks

3 tablespoons plain (all-purpose) flour

½ teaspoon salt

½ teaspoon ground black pepper

1 large onion, peeled and chopped

4 garlic cloves, peeled and minced

2 tablespoons tomato purée (paste)

4 tablespoons brandy or whisky

1 tablespoon Worcestershire sauce

1 litre (4¼ cups) beef stock

300g (4 cups) chestnut (cremini) mushrooms, thickly sliced

1 tablespoon cornflour (cornstarch) mixed with 3 tablespoons cold water to make a slurry (optional)

120ml (½ cup) double (heavy) cream

to serve

chopped flat-leaf parsley

mashed potato

green vegetables, such as broccoli

1. Preheat the oven to 160°C/320°F/gas mark 4.

2. Heat the oil in a large casserole pan over a high heat.

3. Place the beef in a bowl and toss with the flour, salt and pepper to coat.

4. Add the beef to the casserole pan and cook for 6–8 minutes, turning regularly until browned all over (you can do this in batches if you like, but I find it doesn't impact the look or taste if you cook it all in one go).

5. Once the meat is browned, turn the heat down to medium and add the onion. Continue to cook for a further 3–4 minutes, stirring regularly until the onion starts to soften.

6. Stir in the garlic and tomato purée, cook for a further minute, then add the brandy/whisky, Worcestershire sauce, beef stock and mushroom.

7. Stir everything together, being sure to scrape any bits that may have stuck to the bottom of the pan – this adds so much flavour.

8. Bring to the boil, stir again, then cover the pan with a lid and transfer to the oven to cook for 3 hours, until the beef is tender. Check a few times during the final hour of cooking to ensure the casserole doesn't cook dry. If so, add a good splash of boiling water.

9. Once the meat is tender, remove from the oven. If you'd like to thicken the sauce a little, stir in the cornflour slurry.

10. Add the cream and stir, then top with freshly chopped parsley.

11. Serve with mashed potato and green veg, such as broccoli.

TIP You can use a slow cooker instead of the oven. Once you've brought the casserole to the boil, transfer the contents to your slow cooker and cook on high for 5–6 hours, or low for 7–8 hours.

MAKE AHEAD Make the casserole, then cool, cover and refrigerate. Reheat, covered, in the oven at 160°C/320°F/gas mark 3 for 35–45 minutes, until piping hot throughout. Stir once or twice during this time to ensure it heats evenly.

Slow-cooked

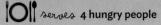
Slow-cooker beef short ribs with gravy

Put these beef short ribs in the slow cooker in the morning, and by tea time you'll have luscious fall-apart beef. All served with a rich and meaty red wine gravy.

1 tablespoon sunflower oil

4 meaty beef short ribs

1 onion, peeled and chopped

3 garlic cloves, peeled and minced

240ml (1 cup) red wine

640ml (2¾ cups) beef stock

1 teaspoon dried thyme

1 tablespoon tomato purée
  (paste)

1 teaspoon sugar

2 bay leaves

¼ teaspoon salt

¼ teaspoon ground black pepper

1 tablespoon Worcestershire
  sauce

2 tablespoons cornflour
  (cornstarch) mixed with
  5 tablespoons cold water
  to a slurry

to serve

creamy mashed potato

green vegetables, such as
  cabbage, broccoli and peas

1. Heat the oil in a large frying pan (skillet) over a high heat.

2. Place the short ribs in the pan and brown on all sides. This should take about 10 minutes.

3. Turn the heat down to medium, add the onion and cook for a further 2 minutes, whilst stirring.

4. Add the garlic and heat through for a minute, then add the red wine. Bring to a bubble and allow to simmer for 3–4 minutes.

5. Add the beef stock, thyme, tomato purée, sugar, bay leaves, salt, pepper and Worcestershire sauce.

6. Bring to the boil, then transfer to the slow cooker. Place the lid on and cook on low for 6–8 hours, until the beef is very tender.

7. To make the gravy, ladle most of the cooking liquid out of the slow cooker and into a saucepan.

8. Slowly stirring with a whisk, over a high heat, pour the cornflour slurry into the cooking liquid, until the gravy thickens. You may not need all of the cornflour slurry. You're looking for a medium-thick gravy.

9. Serve the short ribs with the gravy. I love mine also with mashed potato and green vegetables.

TIP Any leftovers make the basis for fantastic burritos (I heat up the shredded meat and gravy in a pan with a little chilli sauce).

MAKE AHEAD Once cooked, cool quickly in the cooking liquid (do this before making the gravy), then cover and refrigerate for up to 2 days. Reheat in a covered pan (with the cooking liquid)in the oven at 160°C/320°F/ gas mark 4 for 30–40 minutes, until piping hot throughout. Reheating in the liquid will help keep the meat moist. You may need to add a little more stock to ensure you have enough to make gravy once the meat has heated through.

Slow-cooked

Thai-style peanut pork

This simple Thai-inspired Peanut Pork is all cooked in one pan, with the oven doing most of the work. The pork is slow-cooked in a delicious spiced peanut sauce, until it's fall-apart tender, then it's finished off with fresh beansprouts and coriander.

1 tablespoon sunflower oil

1kg (2¼lb) diced pork shoulder

1 onion, peeled and chopped

2 tablespoons ground coriander

1 tablespoon ground cumin

1 teaspoon ground ginger

¼ teaspoon garlic salt

300ml (1¼ cups) chicken stock

1 x 400ml (14oz) can milk

2 heaped tablespoons smooth
    peanut butter

2 tablespoons fish sauce

juice of 1 lime (about 2 tablespoons)

100g (1 cup) beansprouts (fresh,
    or canned beansprouts that
    have been drained)

to serve

cooked rice

fresh coriander (cilantro),
    roughly torn

lime wedges

green chillies, finely chopped

1. Preheat the oven to 170°C/ 325°F/gas mark 5.

2. Heat the oil in a large casserole pan over a high heat until hot.

3. Add the pork and brown on all sides – it should take 6–8 minutes.

4. Turn the heat down to medium and cook the onion for 5 minutes, stirring regularly, until softened.

5. Stir in the ground coriander, cumin, ginger and garlic salt.

6. Add the stock, coconut milk, peanut butter and fish sauce. Stir and bring to a gentle simmer.

7. Cover the pan with a lid and transfer to the oven to cook for 1¾–2 hours, until the pork is fall apart tender. Check a couple of times in the final hour. If it's looking a little dry, stir in a splash of water.

8. Once the pork is tender, remove from the oven and stir in the lime juice, then add the beansprouts.

9. Stir and return to the oven for 10 minutes.

10. Remove from the oven and stir. Serve over cooked rice, garnished with fresh coriander and lime wedges. Add some chopped fresh chillies if you like a bit of heat.

TIP I find that pork shoulder works well in this dish as it has a nice bit of fat running through it, which renders down as it's cooking and becomes really tender and juicy.

MAKE AHEAD Make the dish, without the beansprouts, then cool quickly, cover and refrigerate for up to 2 days. To reheat, add to a saucepan with the beansprouts and reheat over a medium heat, stirring occasionally, until piping hot throughout. Adding the beansprouts only when reheating ensures they retain a slight crunch.

Slow-cooked

165

Slow-cooker smothered pork

This is a lovely tender pork dish with loads of mushrooms and plenty of sauce.
It tastes great over mashed potato or served alongside a baked potato.

3 tablespoons olive oil

4 thick boneless pork shoulder
   or loin steaks

¼ teaspoon salt

½ teaspoon ground black pepper

1 large onion, peeled and thinly
   sliced

3 garlic cloves, peeled and minced

2 tablespoons plain (all-purpose)
   flour

360ml (1½ cups) chicken stock

200g (7oz) mushrooms, sliced

½ tablespoon tomato purée
   (paste)

½ tablespoon white wine vinegar

60ml (¼ cup) double (heavy)
   cream

to serve

2 tablespoons chopped flat-leaf
   parsley

mashed potato

green vegetables, such as sprouts

1. Heat 2 tablespoons of the oil in a large frying pan (skillet) over a high heat.

2. Sprinkle both sides of the pork steaks with the salt and half the pepper.

3. Place the steaks in the pan and fry for 2 minutes on each side, until browned, then transfer to the slow cooker.

4. Add the remaining oil to the pan, turn the heat down to medium and fry the onion for 5 minutes, stirring often, until softened.

5. Add the garlic and fry for a further minute, whilst stirring.

6. Sprinkle the flour over the onion and garlic and stir to coat.

7. Slowly pour in the stock, whilst stirring.

8. Pour the liquid from the pan into the slow cooker.

9. Add the sliced mushroom, tomato purée, white wine vinegar and remaining pepper to the slow cooker. Stir together.

10. Place the lid on and cook on high for 3–4 hours, or low for 5–6 hours.

11. Remove the lid and stir in the cream, then serve topped with a sprinkling of fresh parsley.

12. I like to serve mine with mashed potato and sprouts.

TIP Add some vegetables too, if you like. Chunks of potato, courgette (zucchini), baby carrots and green beans all make a great addition.

Slow-cooked

Creamy slow-cooked pork casserole

Tender pork cooked in a creamy cider and mushroom sauce, all topped off with crispy bacon lardons. This is one of my favourite winter comfort food meals!

2 tablespoons sunflower oil

500g (1lb 2oz) diced pork shoulder

¼ teaspoon salt

¼ teaspoon ground black pepper

¼ teaspoon celery salt

1 onion, peeled and chopped

12 baby mushrooms, cut in half

2 carrots, peeled and roughly chopped

250ml (1 cup + 2 teaspoons) dry (hard) cider

420ml (1¾ cups) chicken stock

½ teaspoon dried thyme

150g (½ cup) bacon lardons

1 tablespoon cornflour (cornstarch) mixed with 3 tablespoons cold water to make a slurry

60ml (¼ cup) double (heavy) cream

chopped flat-leaf parsley, to serve

1. Preheat the oven to 170°C/ 325°F/gas mark 5.

2. Heat 1½ tablespoons of the oil in a large ovenproof casserole dish until hot.

3. In a bowl, toss the pork with the salt, pepper and celery salt, then add to the pan and brown on all sides – it should take 6–8 minutes.

4. Turn the heat down to medium and add the onion. Cook for 5 minutes, stirring occasionally, until it softens.

5. Add the mushrooms and cook for a further 2 minutes, then add the carrot, cider, stock and dried thyme.

6. Turn up the heat and bring to the boil. Stir and scrape any bits than may have stuck to the bottom of the pan – it adds so much flavour.

7. Cover the pan with a lid and place in the oven for 2½–3 hours, until the pork breaks apart when you press it with a fork. Check a couple of times during the final hour of cooking and add a splash of water or stock if it's starting to look a little dry.

8. Ten minutes before the casserole comes out of the oven, heat the remaining ½ tablespoon oil in a frying pan (skillet) over a medium-high heat and fry the

bacon lardons until crispy. Turn off the heat.

9. Remove the casserole from the oven and stir in the cornflour slurry, to thicken, then stir in the cream.

10. Sprinkle over the bacon lardons and a little chopped parsley before serving.

11. I love to serve this with green veg and mashed potato or chunks of crusty bread.

TIP Want to use your slow cooker? Add the casserole to the slow cooker at the point you would be putting it in the oven. Cook for 6–8 hours on low, or 4–5 hours on high.

MAKE AHEAD You can make this dish ahead, then cool, cover and refrigerate for up to a day. Heat through thoroughly in the oven (covered) at 175°C/350°F/ gas mark 6 for approx. 20–25 minutes. Or heat through on the hob (stovetop) over a medium heat for 10–15 minutes, until the pork is hot all the way through. Add a splash of stock or water to loosen it up, if needed.

Slow-cooked

169

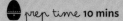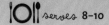
Slow-cooker steamed jam sponge

A slow cooker isn't just for savoury food – you can use it for dessert too! This is a lovely dense sponge, topped with plenty of warm, oozy raspberry jam. Finish off with a good drizzle of cream or custard and you've got a pud that'll take you right back to your childhood!

½ teaspoon soft unsalted butter, for greasing

180g (6⅓oz) unsalted butter, softened

180g (1 cup minus 1 tablespoon) caster (superfine) sugar

3 medium eggs

1 tablespoon milk

1 teaspoon vanilla extract

180g (1½ cups) plain (all-purpose) flour

2 teaspoons baking powder

7 tablespoons raspberry jam

1. Preheat the slow cooker, on the high setting.

2. Grease the inside of a 1.2 litre (2 pint) pudding basin (ovenproof bowl) with butter and set aside.

3. In a large bowl, cream together the butter and sugar until light and creamy (or you can use a stand mixer with a paddle).

4. Add the eggs, one at a time, whilst stirring (don't worry if the mixture looks like it's split – it will come back together).

5. Stir in the milk and vanilla extract, then fold in the flour and baking powder.

6. Spoon the jam into the bottom of your greased pudding basin (bowl), then carefully spoon the cake mixture (batter) on top.

7. Cover the top of the pudding basin with a layer of baking parchment. Fold a pleat across the centre, so there's a little room for the pudding to expand.

8. Secure the pleated parchment with a piece of string tied tightly under the rim of the pudding basin, and cut off any excess parchment paper.

9. Place the pudding, parchment-side-up, in the slow cooker and pour boiling water (from the kettle) into the slow-cooker bowl, so it comes about three-quarters of the way up the sides of the pudding basin.

10. Place the lid on the slow cooker and cook on high for 2½ hours.

11. Once cooked, carefully lift out the pudding basin and remove the string and parchment (be careful, as steam will escape as the paper is taken off).

12. Place an upside-down plate on top of the pudding basin and carefully invert, turning the jam sponge out onto the plate.

13. Serve topped with cream, custard or ice cream.

TIP Swap out the raspberry jam for different flavours – strawberry jam or even marmalade work great!

Slow-cooked

170

Restaurant favourites.

I love going out for dinner, and it always gives me so much inspiration and energy for cooking at home. These are some of my favourite dishes that I've recreated in my own kitchen. My **Tuscan-style chicken** is one of the most popular recipes on our YouTube channel, with so much flavour and lots of lovely sauce! The **Chicken à la King** is a recipe my mum used to make, and I've been making it for over 20 years – it always takes me straight back to my childhood. My **Deep-dish apple pie** took a lot of testing to get just right – with the perfect sweet-yet-tangy flavour. A slice of this pie with a nice dollop of ice cream and you'll be in dessert heaven.

Creamy tomato risotto with garlic crumbs

A bit of a change from regular risotto, this is a creamy tomato version with just a little bit of a tang. I love to top it with easy-to-make garlic breadcrumbs, which add a lovely crunch. Every bite is utterly moreish!

1 x 400g (14oz) can finely chopped tomatoes

240ml (1 cup) vegetable stock

2 tablespoons tomato purée (paste)

1 tablespoon olive oil

1 small onion, peeled and finely chopped

1 garlic clove, peeled and minced

150g (¾ cup) Arborio rice

80ml (⅓ cup) white wine

3 tablespoons double (heavy) cream

4 tablespoons grated Parmesan

1 tablespoon lemon juice

¼ teaspoon salt

¼ teaspoon ground black pepper

garlic crumbs

1 tablespoon unsalted butter

¼ teaspoon Maldon salt (or just a good pinch of normal salt)

2 garlic cloves, peeled and minced

4 tablespoons panko breadcrumbs

1 teaspoon chopped flat-leaf parsley

zest of ½ lemon

3 tablespoons grated Parmesan

1. First make your tomato-based stock. Place the canned tomato in a saucepan, add the vegetable stock and tomato purée and heat until the mixture is almost boiling, then turn off the heat.

2. Heat the oil in a large frying pan (skillet) and cook the onion for about 5 minutes, stirring often, until it starts to soften.

3. Add the garlic, stir and cook for a further minute.

4. Add the rice and stir until the oil has coated the rice.

5. Add the wine and stir.

6. Wait for the wine to be almost fully absorbed (stirring regularly) and then add the tomato stock, a ladle at a time, ensuring each ladle has been almost fully absorbed before adding the next. Ensure you stir regularly.

7. After about 15–20 minutes, you should have used up all the stock. Have a taste of the rice. It should be softer, but still have a slight bite to it (it will soften up further when you add the cream). If the rice is still too hard, you can add in a ladle or so of water and cook for another couple of minutes.

8. While your risotto is cooking, make your crispy garlic crumbs.

9. Heat the butter in a small frying pan until it starts to foam slightly.

10. Add the salt and garlic and cook, stirring, for about 30 seconds.

11. Add the breadcrumbs and stir to ensure they are evenly coated with butter.

12. Allow to cook, stirring often, until the breadcrumbs start to brown a little. Keep a close eye on them as they burn very easily. When browned, turn off the heat and stir in the parsley, lemon zest and Parmesan.

13. Now go back to your risotto. Add in the cream, Parmesan, lemon juice and salt and pepper. Give everything a good stir, then turn off the heat.

14. Spoon the crispy breadcrumbs on top of the risotto and serve.

MAKE IT VEGETARIAN
Simply replace the Parmesan with vegetarian Parmesan (or vegetarian Italian-style hard cheese).

Pan-fried plaice with brown shrimp

I grew up in Southport, where brown shrimp are caught locally, so these juicy little morsels will always have a special place in my heart. Use them to top any pan-fried fish for an extra-special finish!

1 tablespoon olive oil

2 tablespoons unsalted butter

2 plaice (flounder) fillets

¼ teaspoon salt

¼ teaspoon ground black pepper

¼ teaspoon paprika

1 garlic clove, peeled and minced

70g (2½oz) brown shrimp

1 tablespoon lemon juice

3 tablespoons finely chopped
   flat-leaf parsley

to serve

baby new potatoes

green vegetables, such as
   broccoli, cabbage and peas

1. Heat the oil and butter in a frying pan (skillet), over a medium-high heat, until the butter melts.

2. Season the plaice fillets with the salt, pepper and paprika.

3. Add the plaice fillets to the pan, skin-side up, and cook for 2–3 minutes, until browned, then turn over.

4. Add the garlic and brown shrimp to the pan and stir into the butter. Cook for 2–3 minutes, until the brown shrimp are hot throughout.

5. Turn off the heat, then drizzle over the lemon juice and stir in half of the fresh parsley.

6. Arrange the fish on two plates and spoon over the shrimp and any pan juices. Sprinkle over the remaining parsley.

7. I love to serve this with new potatoes and green vegetables.

TIP Don't fancy plaice? Swap it for lemon sole, skate or sea bass.

Restaurant favourites

176

Salmon with creamy white wine sauce

Tender, fall-apart pan-fried salmon in a rich, creamy, white wine and garlic sauce.
All cooked in one pan, this dish has a few little extras to make the sauce over-the-top tasty.
On the table in 15 minutes, it's a great meal when you need dinner fast,
but you want something special.

1 tablespoon sunflower oil
2 skin-on salmon fillets
1 garlic clove, peeled and minced
60ml (¼ cup) white wine
60ml (¼ cup) strong chicken
  stock
180ml (¾ cup) double (heavy)
  cream
¼ teaspoon salt
¼ teaspoon ground black pepper
3 tablespoons grated Parmesan
zest of 1 lemon
1 tablespoon chopped flat-leaf
  parsley

to serve
baby new potatoes
green vegetables, such as broccoli

1. Heat the oil in a frying pan (skillet) over a high heat.

2. Add the salmon, skin-side down, and cook for 2 minutes.

3. Turn the salmon and cook for a further 2 minutes, until lightly browned, then turn back over so it's skin-side down again.

4. Turn the heat down to medium, add the garlic, stir for 30 seconds (no longer or the garlic may burn), then add the white wine.

5. Bring to the boil and allow to bubble for a minute, then pour in the chicken stock. Allow to bubble for a further minute.

6. Add the cream, salt, pepper and Parmesan and bring back to the boil. Simmer gently for a further 3–4 minutes until the sauce is slightly thickened and the salmon is cooked through.

7. Stir in the lemon zest, then serve the salmon topped with a sprinkling of fresh parsley.

8. Serve with baby new potatoes and broccoli.

TIP Skin-on or skinless fillets? I would always suggest going for skin-on salmon fillets as the skin helps to protect the salmon from overcooking and drying out. Once the salmon is cooked, you can easily remove the skin, if you prefer. It will peel right off.

Restaurant favourites

Tuscan-style chicken

Perfectly seasoned pan-fried chicken breasts in a creamy sun-dried tomato sauce with lots of peppers and spinach. It's the ultimate chicken dinner!
Serve with pasta, potatoes or just a big hunk of bread to dip into that creamy sauce.

1 large egg

3 tablespoons plain (all-purpose) flour

¼ teaspoon salt

½ teaspoon ground black pepper

½ teaspoon dried oregano

½ teaspoon dried thyme

½ teaspoon paprika

¼ teaspoon garlic salt

4 chicken breasts

3 tablespoons olive oil

sauce

1 onion, peeled and sliced

2 garlic cloves, peeled and minced

½ teaspoon dried oregano

1 teaspoon paprika

160g (1 cup) sun-dried tomatoes (I like the bright red ones from the deli counter)

1 red (bell) pepper, sliced

1 tablespoon tomato purée (paste)

90ml (⅓ cup) white wine

240ml (1 cup) chicken stock

a pinch of salt and pepper

90ml (⅓ cup) double (heavy) cream

50g (½ cup) grated Parmesan

90g (3 packed cups) baby spinach

1 tablespoon chopped flat-leaf parsley

1. Preheat the oven to 160°C/ 320°F/gas mark 4.

2. Whisk the egg lightly in a shallow bowl.

3. In a separate shallow bowl, mix together the flour, salt, pepper, oregano, thyme, paprika and garlic salt.

4. Dip the chicken breasts first in the egg, then dredge in the flour mixture, until thoroughly coated.

5. Heat 2 tablespoons of the olive oil in a large frying pan (skillet) over a medium-high heat and fry the chicken on both sides until golden.

6. Transfer the chicken to a tray and place in the oven for 10 minutes.

7. Meanwhile, add the remaining tablespoon of oil to the pan, place over a medium heat and cook the onion for 3–4 minutes, until it starts to soften.

8. Add the garlic, oregano, paprika, sun-dried tomato, red pepper and tomato purée. Cook for 2 minutes, stirring.

9. Pour in the wine and allow to bubble for 2 minutes.

10. Add the chicken stock, season, bring to the boil, then simmer for 5 minutes.

11. Add the cream, Parmesan and spinach and stir. Cook for a couple of minutes until the spinach wilts.

12. Remove the chicken from the oven. Check it's cooked all the way through (insert a knife into the fattest piece – it should no longer be pink), then add to the pan and drizzle over the sauce.

13. Serve topped with a sprinkling of fresh parsley. It tastes great with pasta, courgetti (zoodles), rice or sauté potatoes.

TIP I like to cook an extra chicken breast with this dish, then shred/ chop the chicken and serve with a salad for lunch the next day. Way tastier than plain chicken.

MAKE AHEAD Make the dish, then cool, cover and refrigerate for up to a day. Reheat, covered, in the oven at 160°C/320°F/ gas mark 4 for 20–25 minutes, or on the hob (stovetop), until the chicken is piping hot throughout. The sauce thickens when it cools so you may need a splash of water/stock/cream to loosen it up.

Chicken with creamy mushroom sauce

Pan-fried chicken in a creamy white wine and garlic sauce with mushrooms. I love this for a luxury dinner, served with sautéed potatoes and greens. Ready in 25 minutes, it makes a tasty and impressive date-night dinner or a lovely alternative to a Sunday roast.

2 teaspoons sunflower oil

4 chicken breasts

½ teaspoon salt

½ teaspoon pepper

1 small onion, peeled and finely chopped

8 chestnut (cremini) mushrooms, sliced

3 garlic cloves, peeled and minced

¼ teaspoon dried thyme or 2 sprigs fresh thyme

120ml (½ cup) white wine

120ml (½ cup) chicken stock

180ml (¾ cup) double (heavy) cream

to serve

green beans

sauté potatoes

fresh thyme

1. Heat the oil in a large frying pan (skillet) over a medium-high heat.

2. Season both sides of the chicken breasts with salt and pepper, then cook in the pan until golden on both sides (about 6–8 minutes). They don't need to be cooked through at this point – they'll continue cooking in the sauce.

3. Add the onion and mushroom to the pan and cook for 3 minutes, until lightly softened.

4. Stir in the garlic and thyme and cook for 30 seconds.

5. Add the wine and turn the heat up to high. Bring to the boil, then simmer until almost all of the liquid has evaporated (this will take about 5 minutes).

6. Stir in the stock and cream and heat through for 2–3 minutes.

7. Check the chicken is cooked (insert a knife into the fattest piece – it should no longer be pink), then turn off the heat and divide the chicken among four plates.

8. Spoon over the sauce and serve with your choice of sides (I love green beans and sauté potatoes with this dish). Sprinkle over the fresh thyme and serve.

MAKE AHEAD Make the dish, then cool, cover and refrigerate for up to a day. Reheat, covered, in the oven at 160°C/320°F/gas mark 4 for 20–25 minutes, or on the hob (stovetop), until the chicken is piping hot throughout. You may need a splash of stock or cream to loosen it up as it will be a little thicker after cooling.

Restaurant favourites

Chicken à la King

An absolute classic! I've been making this Chicken à la King for years. The recipe was handed down to me from my mum, who used to make it for me when I was growing up.
I love the way the sauce sinks into the rice, making every bite taste creamy, savoury and delicious.

3 tablespoons olive oil

12 baby chestnut (cremini) mushrooms, sliced in half (you can swap for button mushrooms, or 5–6 regular-size sliced mushrooms)

1 large onion, peeled and sliced

2 tablespoons plain (all-purpose) flour

280ml (1 cup + 3 tablespoons) hot chicken stock

200ml (¾ cup + 1 tablespoon) milk

½ teaspoon dried thyme or 1 teaspoon fresh thyme leaves

2 tablespoons dry sherry, carefully measured (too much will make the sauce taste of sherry)

¼ teaspoon salt

¼ teaspoon ground black pepper

2 large, cooked chicken breasts, shredded or chopped into bite-size chunks (about 250g/9oz)

to serve
cooked rice or pasta
chopped flat-leaf parsley

1. Heat 1½ tablespoons of the oil in a large frying pan (skillet) over a medium-high heat.

2. Add the mushroom, cook for about 3–4 minutes until golden brown, then transfer to a bowl and set aside.

3. Heat the remaining 1½ tablespoons of oil in the pan and fry the onion for 5–6 minutes over a medium-high heat, until the edges start to brown slightly. Move the onion around the pan to ensure it doesn't burn.

4. Stir in the flour and cook, stirring, for a minute.

5. Add a splash of the hot stock and mix into the onion/flour with a whisk. It should form a thick paste.

6. Add the rest of the stock, a large splash at a time, and keep stirring with the whisk to ensure the sauce doesn't go lumpy.

7. Once all the stock is incorporated, add the milk and thyme. Keep stirring and the sauce will thicken as it heats up.

8. Once thickened, add the sherry and season with salt and pepper. Give it a taste and add a little more seasoning if needed.

9. Add the cooked chicken, return the mushroom to the pan and stir. Cook for 2–3 minutes to ensure the chicken is hot throughout.

10. Serve on top of some fluffy white rice and finish with a sprinkling of parsley.

TIP You don't have to use chicken breast meat. This dish is great for using up any leftover shreds of cooked chicken. Alternatively, use ready-cooked rotisserie chicken.

Restaurant favourites

Peri-peri chicken

This chicken is juicy, spicy and loaded with flavour, and because it's spatchcocked (butterflied), it cooks in super-quick time! The peri-peri sauce is so good that you'll want to smother it on everything.

peri-peri sauce

2 red (bell) peppers, sliced into large pieces

2 red onions, peeled and chopped into large chunks

120ml (½ cup) sunflower oil,

1 teaspoon paprika

1 teaspoon smoked paprika

2 teaspoons cayenne pepper

1 teaspoon salt

4 garlic cloves, peeled

2 red serrano chillies, deseeded and sliced in half

10 dried African bird's eye chillies

¼ teaspoon white pepper

zest and juice of 1 lemon

¼ teaspoon dried rosemary

4 tablespoons red wine vinegar

1 medium chicken (1.4–1.6kg/ 3–3½lb)

½ teaspoon salt

½ teaspoon ground black pepper

1. Preheat the oven to 180°C/ 350°F/gas mark 6.

2. Place the peppers and onion on a baking tray (sheet). Drizzle over 2 tablespoons of the sunflower oil, sprinkle over the paprika, smoked paprika, cayenne pepper and salt and toss together to coat.

3. Place in the oven for 20 minutes.

4. Add the garlic and chillies to the tray and toss together again, then return the tray to the oven for a further 10 minutes.

5. Remove from the oven and transfer everything to a blender (make sure you pour in all the juices from the tray). Add the dried chillies, white pepper, lemon zest and juice and the dried rosemary. Blend until smooth.

6. Add the remaining sunflower oil and the red wine vinegar and blend again.

7. Now it's time to spatchcock (butterfly) the chicken. Place the chicken, breast-side down, on a sturdy chopping (cutting) board, with the legs toward you.

8. Using heavy-duty scissors or poultry shears, cut along both sides of the backbone. It's a little fiddly, as you have to cut through each of the rib bones as you go. Take your time and go slow; don't try to cut through multiple ribs at once.

9. Once you've cut through both sides of the backbone, discard the bone (or save it to make stock). Turn the chicken over and press down with both hands on the breast bone to flatten the chicken.

10. Place the spatchcocked chicken on a baking tray, breast-side up, pour over one-third of the sauce and sprinkle with the salt and black pepper.

11. Place in the oven (still at 180°C/350°F/gas mark 6) for 45 minutes.

12. After 45 minutes, baste the chicken and spoon over 2 more tablespoons of the sauce. Return to the oven for a further 10–15 minutes, until the chicken is cooked through.

13. Remove from the oven and allow to rest for 10 minutes.

14. Serve with the remaining sauce.

TIP Covered and refrigerated, the peri-peri sauce should keep for 2 weeks.

Restaurant favourites

Slow-cooked lamb shanks with rich sauce

Cooking lamb shanks over 7 or 8 hours in the slow cooker results in beautiful fall-apart meat. We're cooking them with stock, red wine and red currant jelly for a fantastic rich sauce.

2 tablespoons sunflower oil

4 lamb shanks

½ teaspoon salt

½ teaspoon ground black pepper

1 large onion, peeled and
   finely chopped

2 carrots, peeled and chopped
   into small chunks

3 garlic cloves, peeled and minced

240ml (1 cup) red wine

640ml (2¾ cups) lamb stock

½ teaspoon dried thyme

2 tablespoons tomato purée
   (paste)

1 teaspoon sugar

2 bay leaves

2 tablespoons red current jelly

2 tablespoons cornflour
   (cornstarch) mixed with
   5 tablespoons cold water
   to make a slurry

to serve

mashed potato

green vegetables, such as
   asparagus and green beans

a few sprigs of thyme

1. Heat the oil in a large frying pan (skillet) over a high heat.

2. Season the lamb shanks all over with salt and pepper, then place in the pan and brown on all sides. This should take about 10 minutes.

3. Remove from the pan and place the lamb in the slow cooker.

4. Add the onion and carrot to the frying pan and cook for 5 minutes, stirring often, until softened.

5. Add the garlic and cook for a further minute, whilst stirring.

6. Add the red wine, stock, thyme, tomato purée, sugar and bay leaves to the frying pan and bring to a simmer.

7. Turn off the heat and pour the sauce over the lamb shanks in the slow cooker.

8. Place the lid on and cook on low for 7–8 hours, until the lamb is very tender.

9. Once cooked, remove the lamb shanks from the slow cooker. Remove and discard the bay leaves, and stir the red currant jelly into the sauce.

10. To thicken the sauce, slowly pour in the cornflour slurry, whilst stirring with a whisk, until thickened to your liking.

11. I like to serve my lamb shanks on top of mashed potato, with some green vegetables.

12. Pour the sauce over the lamb shanks, sprinkle over the fresh thyme and serve.

TIP You can cook this in the oven if you wish. Instead of transferring to the slow cooker, transfer to a large casserole pan. Cover with a lid and cook in the oven at 180°C/350°F/gas mark 6 for 3–3½ hours. Check during the last hour of cooking and add an extra splash of stock, if needed.

Restaurant favourites

Beef Stroganoff

Rich and indulgent Beef Stroganoff with rib-eye steak and mushrooms is a real treat dinner. Lots of people add mustard and/or brandy to Stroganoff, but this is the version I grew up with – made with sour cream and double cream – and I think it's perfect. It's also ready in less than 20 minutes!

1 tablespoon unsalted butter

2 tablespoons olive oil

1 onion, peeled and finely sliced

200g (3 cups) baby chestnut (cremini) mushrooms, thickly sliced

400g (14oz) fillet (beef tenderloin) or rib-eye steak, sliced into strips, 1cm (½in) thick

¼ teaspoon salt

¼ teaspoon ground black pepper

240ml (1 cup) double (heavy) cream

160ml (⅔ cup) sour cream

to serve

cooked rice or pasta

¼ teaspoon paprika

chopped flat-leaf parsley

1. Heat the butter and half the oil in a large frying pan (skillet) over a medium-high heat, until the butter starts to foam.

2. Add the onion, and cook for 5 minutes, stirring often, until it starts to soften.

3. Add the mushroom and cook for a further 3–4 minutes, stirring often, until lightly browned.

4. Transfer the contents of the pan to a bowl. Place the pan back over the heat and turn it up to high.

5. Drizzle the steak strips with the remaining oil and season with salt and pepper.

6. Place the steak in the pan in a single layer and cook for 1 minute, then turn the strips over and cook for a further 30 seconds.

7. Return the onion and mushroom to the pan and turn the heat down to medium.

8. Pour in the double cream, followed by the sour cream. Stir and slowly heat through, until the sauce is hot and just starting to bubble slightly at the edge of the pan (don't let it boil). Turn off the heat.

9. Spoon the Stroganoff over cooked rice or pasta and sprinkle over the paprika and parsley before serving.

TIP Rib-eye, sirloin (porterhouse) or fillet steak (beef tenderloin) are the best cuts for this dish. You're looking for a steak with lots of flavour, that can be cooked quickly over a high heat without becoming chewy.

Restaurant favourites

191

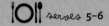
Swedish meatballs

Juicy, flavour-packed meatballs in that classic rich and creamy sauce. This is such a comforting dinner, served with mashed potato and, of course, some lingonberry jam.

500g (1lb 2oz) (ground) beef mince (ideally 20% fat)
250g (9oz) (ground) pork mince
1 onion, peeled and finely chopped
1 garlic clove, peeled and minced
4 tablespoons panko breadcrumbs
1 medium egg
5 tablespoons milk
½ teaspoon salt
¼ teaspoon ground black pepper
¼ teaspoon white pepper
¼ teaspoon allspice
2 tablespoons vegetable or olive oil

sauce
3 tablespoons unsalted butter
3 tablespoons plain (all-purpose) flour
180ml (¾ cup) beef stock
120ml (½ cup) vegetable stock
120ml (½ cup) double (heavy) cream
2 teaspoons dark soy sauce
1 teaspoon Worcestershire sauce
1 teaspoon Dijon mustard
¼ teaspoon salt

to serve
finely chopped flat-leaf parsley
creamy mashed potato
lingonberry jam or red currant jelly
green vegetables, such as broccoli or green beans

1. First make the meatballs. In a large bowl, place the beef mince, pork mince, onion, garlic, breadcrumbs, egg, milk, salt, black pepper, white pepper and allspice.
2. Using your hands, mix it all together, then form into 18–22 meatballs.
3. Preheat the oven to 150°C/ 300°F/gas mark 3.
4. Heat 1 tablespoon of the oil in a large frying pan (skillet) over a medium-high heat until hot.
5. Working in two batches, fry the meatballs in the pan, turning occasionally, until browned all over. Transfer the meatballs to a roasting tray. Use the remaining oil, if needed for the second batch.
6. Place the meatballs in the oven to finish cooking through while you make the sauce (they only need 5–6 minutes).
7. Add the butter to the pan that you cooked the meatballs in and place over a medium heat until it melts.
8. Add the flour and whisk it into the butter to form a roux (thick paste).
9. Add the beef stock, a splash at a time, whilst stirring with the whisk, until fully combined with the butter-flour mixture and no lumps remain.

10. Stir in the vegetable stock and bring to the boil. Add the cream, soy sauce, Worcestershire sauce, mustard and salt and stir to combine.
11. Add the meatballs back to the pan, along with any resting liquid from the tray.
12. Stir to coat the meatballs in the sauce and cook for a further 3–4 minutes, then serve.
13. I like to serve my meatballs with creamy mashed potato, lingonberry jam and green veggies, all topped off with a sprinkling of fresh parsley and black pepper.

MAKE AHEAD Wrap up the meatballs separately from the sauce, cool, cover and refrigerate (or freeze). Reheat on a tray in the oven at 180°C/350°F/gas mark 6 for 20 minutes. Cover them in foil for the first 10 minutes, then remove for the final 10 minutes. Reheat the sauce in a pan until piping hot, then stir in the meatballs.

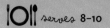
Deep-dish apple pie

This apple pie is filled with lots of layers of apple and warming winter spices. The mixture of two different apple varieties ensures a sweet and tangy flavour and there is just enough sauce to make it saucy, without that dreaded soggy bottom.

3 x 320g (3 x 11oz) packs of ready-rolled shortcrust pastry (pie dough)

5 large Bramley cooking (baking) apples

3 sweet eating apples, such as Jazz or Pink Lady

2 tablespoons lemon juice

3 tablespoons plain (all-purpose) flour

1 tablespoon cornflour (cornstarch)

1 teaspoon ground cinnamon

¼ teaspoon ground ginger

a pinch of ground cloves

150g (¾ cup) light brown sugar

1 teaspoon vanilla extract

1 small egg, lightly whisked

topping
1 tablespoon coarse brown sugar

serve with
ice cream

1. Preheat the oven to 190°C/375°F/gas mark 6.
2. Unroll two of the pastry sheets and use them to line a deep (24cm/9in) pie dish. Don't worry about there being a line where the two pieces meet – just squish them together. You should have some left over. Save this for the top of pie.
3. Place the pastry-lined dish in the refrigerator to chill while you prepare the filling.
4. Peel and core the apples, then slice into 5mm (¼in) thick slices.
5. Place the apple slices in a large bowl and toss with the lemon juice to prevent browning.
6. Add the flour, cornflour, cinnamon, ginger and cloves and toss together to coat the apples. The flour will help ensure a thick sauce in the apple pie.
7. Stir in the sugar and vanilla extract.
8. Arrange the apple mixture into the waiting pie dish. Try to arrange carefully, rather than just emptying them in the pie dish – you want to pack the apple slices, rather than have gaps.
9. Use a sharp knife to trim any pastry that may be hanging over the edge of the dish.

10. Brush the edge of the pie with the egg wash.
11. Unroll the third roll of pastry and slice into long strips, about 2cm (¾in) wide. Slice the leftovers from the second roll too (these can be shorter strips; for the edges of the pie lattice).
12. To make the lattice, arrange strips vertically over the pie, leaving a 5mm (³⁄₁₆in) gap in-between each strip.
13. Fold back every other strip that you've just laid and place a horizontal strip across the top of the pie. Layer the strips you folded back into place, so it looks like you've weaved it together.
14. Repeat, folding back the strips that that weren't folded back previously. Layer another horizontal strip on top, leaving a 5mm (¼in) gap between that strip and the previous strip. Place the folded pastry back into place.
15. Continue this way, weaving until the whole pie is covered.
16. Using a sharp knife, trim off any overhang.
17. Brush all exposed pastry (pie dough) with egg wash.
18. Sprinkle the coarse sugar over the top of the pie.

19. Place in the oven to bake for 55–60 minutes, until the pastry turns deep golden brown. If the pie starts to look too brown after the first 30 minutes, cover with foil. If covering, cook for the full 60 minutes.

20. Remove from the oven and cool for 15 minutes before slicing. Serve with ice cream.

TIP Don't forget to add the lemon juice, as this will stop your apples from going brown. Try to keep your apple slices the same size and remember to pack them in and pile them high!

MAKE AHEAD You can make the pie ahead and serve cool or just slightly warm. Cooling the pie allows the sauce to thicken further, so the apple pie keeps its shape really well when slicing. You can reheat the pie in the oven, covered (190°C/375°F/ gas mark 6) for 10–30 minutes, depending on how much of the pie you're reheating. Don't microwave though as it will make the crust soggy.

Superb Sundays.

One of the first meals I was taught to make was a Sunday dinner. Sounds like a complicated meal to make for a newbie in the kitchen, but I think being thrown in at the deep end really helped me to get to grips with cooking and time management at an early age. Since then, I've learned that Sunday roasts can actually be quite simple – like my easy **Roast chicken** (just one minute of prep!), my **Steamed vegetable medley**, using a two-tiered steam pan to cook five different vegetables at the same time, or my **Best crispy roast potatoes** that can be made ahead. I absolutely love the tradition of a Sunday lunch, with the family round the table.

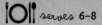
Cheesy vegetable nut roast

A super-flavourful meat-free alternative for your roast dinner.
This nut roast can be sliced and served. Meat-eaters love it too!

300g (10½oz) sweet potato, peeled and chopped into 1cm (½in) cubes
1 tablespoon olive oil
2 tablespoons unsalted butter
1 red onion, peeled and finely chopped
2 garlic cloves, peeled and minced
2 celery sticks, finely diced
¾ teaspoon salt
¾ teaspoon ground black pepper
¼ teaspoon celery salt
1 teaspoon Italian herb mix
1 x 300g (10½oz) can cannellini beans, drained
300g (10½oz) cooked long-grain white rice (approx. 100g/½ cup uncooked weight)
120g (approx. 1 cup) chopped mixed nuts (I use pecans, cashews and hazelnuts)
150g (1½ cups) grated vegetarian Cheddar
75g (1½ cups) panko breadcrumbs
2 tablespoons milk
2 medium eggs
sprigs of thyme, to serve

1. Preheat the oven to 190°C/375°F/gas mark 6 and grease a 1.8kg (4lb) loaf tin (pan).
2. Boil or steam the sweet potato for 10 minutes until tender, then drain.
3. Heat the olive oil and butter in a large frying pan (skillet), over a medium-high heat, until the butter melts.
4. Add the onion and cook for 3 minutes, stirring often, until it starts to soften.
5. Add the garlic and cook for 30 seconds, then add the celery, cooked sweet potato, salt, pepper, celery salt and Italian herb mix.
6. Cook, stirring, for 5 minutes.
7. Turn off the heat, then add the cannellini beans, cooked rice, nuts, cheese, panko breadcrumbs, milk and eggs. Stir together until combined.
8. Transfer the contents of the pan to the prepared loaf tin and push the mixture down with the back of a spoon.
9. Cover the top of the tin with a piece of greased foil, then place in the oven for 45 minutes.

10. After 45 minutes, remove from the oven and leave to cool for 5 minutes, then run a knife around the edge of the loaf tin and turn the contents out onto a plate.
11. Top with sprigs of fresh thyme.
12. Slice the nut roast and serve as part of your roast dinner.

TIP Don't want to use egg? Mix 2 tablespoons ground flaxseed with 6 tablespoons cold water and leave to sit for 15 minutes. Use this mixture as a replacement for the 2 eggs.

Superb Sundays

Roast chicken

It's easy to get carried away, thinking roast chicken needs to be cooked on vegetable trivets, filled with stuffing or bunches of herbs, or requires butter concoctions to put under the skin. Well, I don't agree. For me, simple is best; a bit of seasoning and a lemon wedge in the cavity, and that's all you need for a lovely juicy chicken with seasoned crispy skin, and it takes only 1 minute of prep. That's my aim in life when it comes to a roast chicken.

1 whole chicken, approx. 1½kg (3⅓lb), ideally free-range
1 tablespoon olive oil
½ teaspoon salt
½ teaspoon ground black pepper
¼ teaspoon dried thyme
½ lemon, chopped into 2 wedges (optional)

1. Take the chicken out of the refrigerator 30–45 minutes before roasting to take the chill off it.
2. Preheat the oven to 180°C/350°F/gas mark 6.
3. Place the chicken in a roasting tin (pan). Don't wash it. Drizzle over the oil and, using your hands, rub it into the skin.
4. Sprinkle over the salt, pepper and thyme and place the lemon wedges inside the chicken.
5. Place the chicken in the oven for approx. 80–90 minutes – until the skin is golden and the juices run clear (you can test this by inserting a skewer in the thickest part of the thigh – the liquid that runs out should be clear). If you have a temperature probe, the internal temperature should be 75°C (165°F).
6. Remove the chicken from the oven and leave to rest for 10 minutes on a warm plate before carving and serving.

TIP Who doesn't want crispy skin? If you want the skin to remain crisp, don't cover the chicken during resting. It will still stay warm for 15–20 minutes in a warm kitchen.

One-pan roast leg of lamb with vegetables

This is the easiest way to make a full roast dinner, using only <u>one</u> roasting tin. We add the vegetables in at different times, to ensure everything is finished at the same time. The vegetables are roasted in the oil and the meat juices, so they taste divine!

2kg (4⅓lb) leg of lamb

3 tablespoons olive oil

1 teaspoon salt

1 teaspoon ground black pepper,

½ teaspoon dried rosemary

½ teaspoon dried thyme

4 medium potatoes, scrubbed and chopped into large chunks (no need to peel)

3 carrots, peeled and chopped into bite-size chunks

3 parsnips, peeled and chopped into bite-size chunks

10 large radishes, sliced in half

150g (5½oz) sliced runner (string) beans

100g (3½oz) extra-fine green beans

1. Preheat the oven to 180°C/ 350°F/gas mark 6. Place the lamb in a large roasting tin (pan) and score the fatty bits of the lamb lightly with a sharp knife.

2. Using your hands, rub 1 tablespoon of the olive oil into the meat, then sprinkle over half the salt and pepper, along with the rosemary.

3. Place in the oven for 1 hour 15 minutes.

4. After 1 hour 15 minutes, baste the lamb, then arrange the potato in the tin around the lamb. Drizzle the remaining 2 tablespoons of oil over the potatoes, sprinkle over the thyme and season with (¼ teaspoon each) salt and pepper.

5. Return the lamb to the oven to cook, uncovered, for 15 minutes

6. After 15 minutes, open the oven and turn the potatoes. Add the carrot, parsnip and radish to the tin, turn them in the oil and meat juices to coat, then return to the oven for a further 25 minutes.

7. After 25 minutes, add the runner beans and green beans. Turn to coat in the oil and meat juices and sprinkle the remaining (¼ teaspoon each) salt and pepper over all the vegetables. Return to the oven for a final 15 minutes.

8. Remove from the oven and place the lamb and vegetables on a warm serving plate to serve.

TIP If you want to serve up gravy with this meal, after you've removed the lamb and vegetables, add 300ml (1¼ cups) lamb stock to the juices left in the roasting tin. Place on the hob (stovetop) over a medium heat and bring to the boil, then stir in a cornflour (cornstarch) slurry of 1 tablespoon cornflour, mixed with 2 tablespoons cold water, to thicken.

Roast beef

Keeping it simple is the best way to let the flavour of roasted meat really shine through. Go with a good-quality joint of beef with some fat (not gristle) running through it if possible, and some fat on top. This will help to protect the beef from drying out, ensuring a lovely juicy roasting joint. Whilst beef rib or sirloin (porterhouse) are often the most tender joints, they're also the most expensive, so I usually use topside, which is a good cut of beef that isn't too expensive.

1½kg (3⅓lb) topside of beef
(go for the best quality you
can afford)
1 tablespoon olive oil
½ teaspoon salt
½ teaspoon ground black pepper

1. Preheat the oven to 180°C/ 350°F/gas mark 6.
2. Drizzle the oil over the beef and season with salt and pepper.
3. Transfer to a roasting tin (pan) and place in the oven (uncovered) for 1 hour 15 minutes (for medium) or 1 hour 30 minutes (for well done). Baste once, halfway through cooking.
4. Once cooked, remove the beef from the oven and transfer to a board or warm plate.
5. Allow to rest for 15–20 minutes. If you still have other elements of your roast dinner to make, then cover the beef with foil and a couple of tea (dish) towels – this will allow the meat to rest and keep warm for 30–40 minutes.
6. Reserve any roasting juices and juices from resting the meat to make your gravy (see my recipe on page 209).

TIP Topside is a nice flavourful cut of beef, but is a little on the lean side, so can be less tender than more expensive cuts. Ensure your topside joint has fat on the top (the fat is usually a sheet of fat, added from another part of the cow, but it will still help keep the beef juicy), and be sure to slice it thinly.

Superb Sundays

Roast pork with crackling

Succulent roast pork with perfect crispy crackling (no kidding, it's the best you'll ever eat) and an easy flavour-packed gravy.

roast pork

2.2–2½kg (4¾–5½lb) rolled boneless pork shoulder joint

2 garlic cloves, peeled and minced

1 teaspoon fresh thyme leaves, or ½ teaspoon dried thyme

1 tablespoon finely chopped flat-leaf parsley, or ½ teaspoon dried parsley

¼ teaspoon ground black pepper

1 tablespoon salt

gravy

meat juices from your roasted pork

3 chicken stock cubes, crumbled

720ml (3 cups) boiling water (or vegetable stock from your boiled/steamed vegetables and potatoes if you made some)

¼ teaspoon salt

¼ teaspoon ground black pepper

2 tablespoons cornflour (cornstarch) mixed with 5 tablespoons cold water to make a slurry

¼ teaspoon gravy browning, (optional)

1. Preheat the oven to 170°C/325°F/gas mark 5.

2. Unroll the pork (if it has already been rolled by your butcher) and place on a tray, skin-side up.

3. Using a sharp knife, score the fat in diagonal lines deeply, but not so far as to cut into the meat itself.

4. Turn the pork over. Mix the garlic, thyme, parsley and black pepper together and rub onto the meat and into any grooves.

5. Turn the pork back over so it's skin-side up, then roll and secure with 3–4 pieces of butcher's string.

6. Rub the salt all over the skin.

7. Place the joint on a wire rack over a roasting tin (pan) and roast in the oven for 2½ hours.

8. After 2½ hours, remove from the oven and turn the heat up to 220°C/425°F/gas mark 9.

9. Transfer any meat juices to a saucepan (scraping any crispy bits on the bottom of the tin – you can deglaze with a little water if you need to), then dry off the roasting tin and return the pork to the wire rack set over it.

10. Place the pork back in the oven for 20–25 minutes, turning a couple of times to allow the skin to crisp. Keep a close eye on the joint to ensure the skin doesn't burn.

11. Meanwhile, heat the meat juices in the saucepan and crumble in the stock cubes.

12. Stir together whilst pouring in the hot water (or vegetable cooking water). Bring to the boil and lightly season.

13. Whisk in the cornflour slurry, until the gravy thickens. Stir in the gravy browning, if using. Allow to bubble, then turn off the heat.

14. Remove the pork from the oven and rest for 10 minutes.

15. Once rested, add any meat juices from the rested meat to the gravy and heat it through again. Check the gravy for seasoning.

16. Serve the pork with the gravy, some apple sauce and your favourite vegetables.

TIP It's important to go for a really good-quality joint of pork. Cheaper intensively reared pork can be injected with water (to increase the weight); this produces steam underneath the skin as it cooks, which can make the crackling tough and chewy. I like to use a rolled boneless shoulder joint with a good layer of fat and skin. Shoulder meat has a little fat in the meat (as well as under the skin), so it's really succulent.

Superb Sundays

207

Gravy

FONEG: Fear of not enough gravy! You're last on the table to be handed the gravy jug, and there's only a dribble left. That would be a serious tragedy. It's not cheating to add a couple of stock cubes to the juices from your roasting meat. It will make that gravy go MUCH further. Never suffer FONEG again.

meat juices from your
  roasted meat

2-3 crumbled stock cubes
  (chicken, beef or lamb,
  depending on which meat
  you've cooked, or a mixture of
  chicken and beef for roast pork

720ml (3 cups) hot vegetable
  stock – from your boiled/
  steamed vegetables and
  potatoes

¼ teaspoon salt

¼ teaspoon ground black pepper

2 tablespoons cornflour
  (cornstarch) mixed with
  5 tablespoons cold water, to
  form a slurry

¼ teaspoon gravy browning
  (optional)

1. Heat the meat juices in the roasting tin (pan) over a medium heat. (Ensure it can take direct heat. If not, transfer to a saucepan.)

2. Crumble in the stock cubes and stir together, whilst pouring in the hot vegetable water. Bring to the boil and lightly season with salt and pepper.

3. Using a whisk, stir in the cornflour (cornstarch) slurry, until the gravy thickens.

4. Allow to bubble. Add any meat juices from the rested meat. Check for seasoning and add a little more salt and pepper if needed.

5. If you want the gravy to be a darker brown, stir in the gravy browning.

6. Serve immediately, or turn off the heat until the rest of your roast dinner is ready and reheat just before serving. If you're short on hob (stovetop) space, pour into a microwaveable jug and reheat in the microwave.

TIP Why are we adding stock cubes? If you want lots of gravy, you're going to need some help. The meat juices from your roasting joint will generally have a lovely, deep flavour, but they won't go very far. Adding the vegetable water from steaming/ boiling your vegetables, as well as crumbled up stock cubes will make the gravy stretch much further, whilst still ensuring the flavour from the meat juices shines through.

Easiest cauliflower cheese

This is my easy cauliflower cheese; super-simple, without the need for a béchamel sauce. Less effort, less washing up but still with all the creamy, cheesy flavour!

1 medium cauliflower, broken
  into small florets
240ml (1 cup) double
  (heavy) cream
150g (1½ cups) grated mature
  (sharp) Cheddar
¼ teaspoon salt
½ teaspoon ground black pepper
1 tablespoon finely chopped
  flat-leaf parsley

1. Preheat the oven to 200°C/400°F/gas mark 7.
2. Bring a large pan of water to the boil and simmer the cauliflower florets for 5 minutes, until the cauliflower is tender but not soggy, then drain.
3. Pour 2 tablespoons of the cream in a baking dish and sprinkle over 2 tablespoons of the grated cheese.
4. Add half of the cauliflower, then top with half of the remaining cream and a quarter of the remaining cheese.
5. Season with half of the salt and pepper.
6. Top with the remaining cauliflower, then pour over the remaining cream. Sprinkle over the rest of the cheese, salt and pepper.
7. Place in the oven for 15–20 minutes, until the cheese is golden and bubbly.
8. Remove from the oven and sprinkle with the chopped parsley before serving.

MAKE AHEAD Prepare the cauliflower cheese right up to the point where you put it in the oven. Cool, cover and refrigerate for up to a day. Take out of the refrigerator an hour before baking. Bake in the oven at 200°C/400°F/gas mark 7 for 20–25 minutes, until golden and bubbly.

The best crispy roast potatoes

*The secret to the best crispy potatoes is to boil them long enough so they
REALLY fluff up when you shake the pan.
All of those fluffy bits turn into amazing craggly edges when cooked in hot fat. Perfection.*

1kg (2¼lb) floury potatoes, such
  as Maris Piper or red-skinned
  Rooster potatoes
120g (½ cup) lard or goose fat
  (use sunflower oil instead
  for a vegetarian version)
1 teaspoon Maldon salt
1 tablespoon thyme leaves

1. Preheat the oven to 220°C/
425°F/gas mark 9.
2. Peel the potatoes and chop into
chunky pieces, a little bigger than
a ping pong ball (approx. 5cm/2in
across).
3. Place in a pan and cover with
cold water. Bring to the boil over a
high heat, then turn down the heat
and simmer for 10–11 minutes –
until softened at the edges.
4. Meanwhile, place the lard
(or goose fat, if using) in a large
roasting tin (pan) and place in
the oven for 10 minutes until
shimmering hot.
5. Drain the potatoes in a colander
and give them a good shake to
really roughen up the edges. Don't
worry if a few break apart and they
look overly fluffy. The more fluffy
they are, the better they'll absorb
the fat and the crispier they'll be.
6. Using tongs, carefully transfer
the potatoes to the baking tin with
the hot fat. Turn them over once
to coat in the fat and then place in
the oven.
7. Cook for 30–35 minutes, turning
once or twice in the last 15 minutes
of cooking, until golden and crispy.
8. Remove from the roasting tin
and serve topped with a sprinkling
of Maldon salt and some fresh
thyme leaves.

TIP 10–11 minutes might seem
like a long time to par-boil
potatoes, but it's only after this
amount of time that the potatoes
will be cooked and tender at the
edges. This will allow the edges
to fluff up a lot when shaken, and
it's this that will go extra crispy in
the oven.

MAKE AHEAD Follow the
recipe in the same way, but
just roast the potatoes for
20 minutes or until lightly golden.
Then remove the potatoes from
the fat and place in a bowl to
cool. Cover and refrigerate for
up to a day. Cool and cover the
fat too. When you're ready to
finish the potatoes, heat the fat
in the oven at 220°C/425°F/
gas mark 9 for 10 minutes, then
add the potatoes back in and cook
for 20–30 minutes, turning once,
until golden. This method works
particularly well when you're
cooking for lots of people; having
the potatoes par-roasted means
they should take no longer than
30 minutes to finish off.

Dauphinoise potatoes

Classic dauphinoise potatoes, baked in a creamy garlic sauce and finished with Gruyère cheese. A rich and indulgent side dish that totally hits the spot!

480ml (2 cups) double (heavy) cream

480ml (2 cups) milk

3 garlic cloves, peeled and lightly crushed (so they're flatter, but stay in one piece)

1.25kg (2¾lb) King Edward or Maris Piper potatoes, or other medium-size potatoes

½ teaspoon salt

½ teaspoon ground black pepper

¼ teaspoon ground white pepper

a pinch of nutmeg

150g (1½ cups) grated Gruyère cheese

2 tablespoons chopped flat-leaf parsley

1. Preheat the oven to 190°C/375°F/gas mark 6.

2. Lightly grease a large, shallow ovenproof dish. I use a 32 x 18cm (12 x 7in) dish.

3. Place the cream, milk and garlic in a large saucepan and bring to the boil, then turn down the heat.

4. Peel the potatoes and slice thinly (using the slicing attachment on your food processor or a mandolin). They need to be around 2mm (¹⁄₁₆in) thick.

5. Add the potato to the cream, stir to coat and bring back to the boil.

6. Simmer gently for 6–7 minutes, stirring occasionally (to ensure the sauce doesn't catch on the bottom of the pan) until the potatoes are tender and just cooked. Don't worry if they break apart a little.

7. While the potato is cooking, in a small dish, mix together the salt, peppers and nutmeg.

8. Scoop half of the potato out of the pan and arrange it in the baking dish, being sure to separate any slices that have stuck together. Discard the garlic.

9. Sprinkle over half the salt-pepper-nutmeg mixture and a third of the Gruyère cheese.

10. Layer on the remaining potato and pour over enough sauce to coat the layer but not drown it.

11. Sprinkle over the remaining seasoning and remaining cheese.

12. Place in the oven and bake for 40–45 minutes, until the cheese is golden.

13. Top with fresh parsley.

TIP When par-boiling the potatoes in the sauce, use a blunt knife to separate the layers. The starch in the potatoes means the slices will try to stick together without having any sauce in-between them. This is comparable to not slicing the potatoes at all, and means they won't cook evenly. Separate them out in the pan and ensure all of the slices get coated in the sauce for perfectly tender, creamy potatoes.

MAKE AHEAD Follow the recipe, but cook in the oven for just 20 minutes. Then cool, cover and refrigerate. Remove from the refrigerator an hour before you want to reheat it (to take the chill off the centre) and cover in foil. Place in the oven at 190°C/375°F/gas mark 6 for 30–35 minutes, removing the foil for the last 15 minutes, until piping hot throughout.

MAKE IT VEGETARIAN
Replace the Gruyère with vegetarian Cheddar.

Perfect Yorkshire puddings

My Yorkshire pudding recipe has been tried and tested hundreds of times.
I've been making them this way for years to get lovely big, crispy Yorkshires.

140g (1 cup + 1 tablespoon) plain (all-purpose) flour
4 medium eggs
200ml (¾ cup + 1 tablespoon) semi-skimmed (half-fat) milk
6 teaspoons lard or beef dripping (replace with sunflower oil for a vegetarian version)
¼ teaspoon salt
¼ teaspoon ground black pepper

1. Place the flour in a bowl and make a well in the centre.

2. Add the eggs and, using a balloon whisk, bring the flour into the centre with the eggs, bit by bit.

3. Add the milk and stir again with the whisk until combined. It's fine if it's a little bit lumpy.

4. Place the bowl in the fridge for at least 30 minutes (and up to overnight) to chill. This is important to allow the flour granules to swell (also, cold batter hitting a very hot pan should result in a good rise).

5. Preheat the oven to 220°C/425°F/gas mark 9.

6. Add ½ teaspoon of lard to each hole of a 12-hole metal bun tin. Place in the oven to heat for 10 minutes.

7. Season the Yorkshire pudding batter with salt and pepper and stir once more with a whisk.

8. Open the oven door, pull out the tray and quickly but carefully pour the batter into each of the prepared muffin holes, then close the door immediately and cook for 15–18 minutes, until risen and golden.

TIP Alternatively, you can make 6 large Yorkshire puddings – rather than 12 small ones. Use a large, deep Yorkshire pudding tin. Place 1 teaspoon of lard/dripping in each hole and heat in the oven at 220°C/425°F/gas mark 9 for 10 minutes. Divide the batter among the holes and cook for 25–30 minutes. Turn each Yorkshire pudding over in the pan for the last 5 minutes of cooking to ensure the base is lovely and crisp.

MAKE AHEAD Make the Yorkshire puddings, then cool, place in a sealed freezer bag and freeze. To reheat, remove from the freezer bag and place in the oven (from frozen) at 200°C/400°F/gas mark 7 (5–7 minutes for small ones, 9–12 minutes for large ones), until crispy and hot throughout.

Steamed vegetable medley

Using a two-tiered steamer pan is a great way to steam lots of vegetables, whilst using only one burner on the hob (stovetop). This is a great space saver when you're making a roast dinner, using lots of pots and pans! You can add the vegetables in at different times, depending on the cooking times of each vegetable, so everything will be ready at the same time.

300g (10½oz) Chantenay carrots, scrubbed

1 small head of cauliflower, chopped into florets

1 head of broccoli, chopped into florets

150g (5½oz) asparagus

150g (5½oz) fine green beans

to serve

2 tablespoons salted butter, softened

¼ teaspoon ground white pepper

1 tablespoon finely chopped flat-leaf parsley

1. Fill the base pan of a two-tier steamer pan with 5cm (2in) of water and bring to the boil.

2. Place the first steam basket on top of the pan of water and place the carrots in the steamer basket. Place a lid on the pan, turn the heat down to medium and simmer for 5 minutes.

3. After 5 minutes, add the cauliflower and broccoli to the steam basket and steam for a further 5 minutes.

4. Now add the asparagus and green beans to the second steamer basket and place on top of the first steam basket. Steam both for a final 10 minutes, until all of the vegetables are tender.

5. Whilst the vegetables are steaming, mix together the butter and white pepper.

6. Once cooked, remove the vegetables from the steam baskets and place in a warm serving bowl.

7. Top with the butter (which should melt into the vegetables) and sprinkle over the parsley just before serving.

TIP Use different vegetables, adjusting the time you add them into the steamer, based on their regular cooking time.

Blueberry crumble pie

Can't decide between a fruit pie or a fruit crumble? Why not go with both! This dessert has a shortcrust pastry base and a buttery crumble topping. It's packed full of lovely juicy blueberries. I love it topped with ice cream.

1 x 320g (11oz) pack of ready-rolled shortcrust pastry (pie dough)

180g (1½ cups) plain (all-purpose) flour

1 teaspoon baking powder

115g (4oz) cold unsalted butter, cut into small cubes

60g (¼ cup) white caster (superfine) sugar

60g (¼ cup) light brown sugar

½ teaspoon salt

1 small egg, beaten

1 teaspoon vanilla extract

berry filling

600g (approx. 4 cups) fresh blueberries

120g (½ cup) white caster (superfine) sugar

2 teaspoons lemon juice

1 tablespoon cornflour (cornstarch)

2 tablespoons plain (all-purpose) flour

1. Preheat your oven to 200°C/400°F/gas mark 7.

2. Unroll the shortcrust pastry and use it to line a round 22cm (8½in) pie dish.

3. Trim the edges and use a fork to pierce several holes into the base of the dish.

4. Cover the pastry with a large piece of baking parchment and fill with baking (or dried) beans.

5. Blind bake the pastry in the oven for 20 minutes.

6. Remove the pie dish from the oven, allow to cool a little, then remove the baking (dried) beans and parchment and set aside to cool completely.

7. When the pastry is cool, preheat the oven to 190°C/375°F/gas mark 6.

8. Now make the crumble topping. Place the flour, baking powder and cold butter cubes in a large bowl.

9. Using your fingertips, rub the butter into the flour until the mix resembles breadcrumbs. Don't worry if you have large chunks in there – it adds to the texture.

10. Add the white and brown sugar, along with the salt, egg and vanilla extract, then mix it all together with your hands. You should have some fine crumbly bits and some big clumps.

11. Now make the blueberry mixture. In a medium-size bowl, mix together the blueberries, sugar, lemon juice, cornflour and flour.

12. Spoon the blueberry mixture into the pastry-lined pie dish.

13. Sprinkle the crumble mixture over the top of the blueberries.

14. Place in the oven and cook for 45 minutes. You may need to cover the dish with foil after the first 25 minutes, to prevent the topping from browning too much.

15. Remove from the oven and leave to cool. The pie needs to cool at room temperature for 3–4 hours to allow the blueberry mixture to thicken. If you prefer to serve it warm, you can just leave it to cool for 30 minutes, but the filling will be a lot juicier.

TIP Swap out blueberries for a mixture of apple and blackberry or fresh cherries. If you want to make this recipe even simpler, you can fill with a canned fruit pie filling instead of the blueberry mixture.

Superb Sundays

Index

Acknowledgements

I'm so very grateful that I've been given the opportunity to write the book I really wanted to write and to share my passion for food. Thank you to everyone at Kyle Books, especially Judith Hannam who believed in my vision, and really listened. Thank you also to Samhita Foria (project editor), Helen Bratby (designer), Emily Noto (production), Victoria Scales and Meg Brown (publicity), and everyone else at Kyle.

I'd also like to say a big thank you to my literary agent, Emily Sweet. Emily, I could not have done this without you. You're a mine of information, you provide such valuable input, and you have a brilliant way of bringing everything together.

Thank you to my husband Chris, who has to spend pretty much every minute of the day with me, in the office and at home. You've helped me so much, every step of the way.

To Kath, my mother-in-law, who also works on *Kitchen Sanctuary*, and helps to keep our social media running smoothly – thank you!

To all our readers on the blog, on social media, and also to our watchers on YouTube. Thank you so much for supporting *Kitchen Sanctuary*, for liking, commenting, asking questions, giving feedback, and for coming back again and again to cook our recipes. We appreciate you all so much x